PRAISE FOR

WHAT IS THE GOAL?

"The trickle-down influence of commercialization on youth sports during the past generation has morphed into a waterfall. Jean Linscott and Ken Ruoff have experienced this change and used their clinical and historical perspectives to describe how it has impacted the organization and culture of youth sports as well as the experiences of everyone from program managers to child participants and their families. Reading this book provides a foundation for reclaiming youth sports for young people without breaking family budgets."

—**JAY COAKLEY**, Ph.D., Professor Emeritus, Sociology
Department, University of Colorado at Colorado Springs

"Through exhaustive research and personal experiences, Ken and Jean have truly captured and exposed the issues within the Youth Sports Industry in America. Having been involved with youth sports (specifically soccer) for over 40 years, I have seen first hand how the once "play for fun" mentality has shifted due to the enormous pressure that the youth sports environment places on parents, coaches and clubs. This book is spot on in revealing the challenges that face parents when it comes to deciding on which direction to go with their young participating athletes. If you have a son or daughter that is involved in youth sports, reading this book will help you navigate the delicate landscape of the youth sports culture."

—**DAVE SARACHAN**, longtime professional soccer coach
and interim coach, United States Men's National Team, 2017-18

"*What is the Goal?* drills deep into the labyrinth of contemporary youth sports and exposes it as a hyper-commercialized mechanism of exploitation that suffocates childhood fun. Ruoff and Linscott combine existing research with a wealth of personal examples to meticulously peel back commercialized youth sports' many insidious layers. The book also offers thoughtful and positive suggestions for changing both youth sports and the intercollegiate athletic system that often enables it."

—**RICK ECKSTEIN**, Ph.D. Author, *How College Athletics are Hurting Girls' Sports: The Pay to Play Pipeline*

WHAT IS THE GOAL?

WHAT IS THE GOAL?

The Truth About the Youth Sports Industry

JEAN L. LINSCOTT & KENNETH J. RUOFF

OFFSIDES PRESS

Published in 2024 by Offsides Press

ISBN: 979-8-9901143-0-2
e-ISBN: 979-8-9901143-1-9

Library of Congress Control Number: 2024904661

Cover and interior design: Jenny Kimura
Design services provided by Indigo: Editing, Design, and More

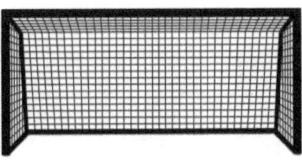

To Patrick, Megan, and Carolyn.
May sports always be a joyous part of your lives.

Table of Contents

Chapter 4: A Road Map for Navigating Pay-to-Play Sports

Chapter 5: How Change Could Happen

Acknowledgments

We are grateful to those friends, family members, coaches, administrators, and authors who helped us better understand the Youth Sports Industry. Our book would not have been possible without their contributions. We thank our children, Carolyn, Megan, and Patrick, for sharing with us their victories, heartbreaks, and struggles during their sporting journeys, and for their willingness to allow us to share some of their stories. They also served as critical editors at various stages of this book's writing.

Louise Damberg was our professional editor. The depth of her professional and life experience allowed Louise to understand our book's purpose, and how to communicate what was most important. She skillfully weeded out academic-speak from our writing, and helped us produce a succinct and readable manuscript. Louise knew how to tame the "mouse who ate the elephant." She listened to our dilemmas and always had a solution for us. She was not afraid to tell us what needed to go and what needed to be redone. Thank you also to Judith Pullan, Jean's long time professional colleague and friend, who introduced us to Louise, and who knew that our passion for this topic needed to be seen to completion.

Cheryl Linscott, USA Swimming coach and Jean's sister, shared invaluable insight as both a nationally respected coach, a deeply respected sister, and a parent with her husband Bob, of five incredible children and athletes. Thank you to our fellow parents of youth athletes who took the time to complete our survey and share your honest impressions. We enjoyed our years spent cheering with you. Thank you also to Pammie Hummelt, Michelle Tubbs, and Janine and David

Segal, parents whose experiences made us think so carefully that we asked to interview them in person. They graciously accepted.

Scot Thompson and Tracy Hasson, two of our children's former coaches, agreed to be interviewed. Scot gave a detailed accounting of the business model for pay-to-play clubs and the numerous ethical challenges one faces as a club director and coach. Tracy helped explain the coaching conflicts related to player development, coach employment, costs to families, and the need for a multitiered system in the youth soccer system.

John O'Sullivan spoke to us about his coaching and writing experiences and how youth sports should be seen as a neutral experience, which can be made into positive or negative experiences by those involved. Jay Coakley, Rick Eckstein, and Mark Hyman, nationally recognized authors on youth sports, encouraged us to see the project to fruition. Over the years, we listened carefully to two of the most respected of our children's coaches, John Bain and Brian Gant. Time, experience, and having nothing to prove helped these men be among the best coaches.

Benjamin Dudley, a local, dedicated representative of the Positive Coaching Alliance, spoke with us at length about alternate models for increasing the accessibility of youth sports. He discussed the barriers to bringing the Positive Coaching Alliance to local pay-to-play clubs, and its limitations when a club's participation in the Positive Coaching Alliance is voluntary and no follow-up or regulation is required.

Nick Gates from Coaches Across Continents, and Ken's teammate from college days, spoke to us at length about how the Youth Sports Industry in the United States differs from how other countries approach player development and facilitate a positive sports experience. Paul Luchowski, a friend and former teammate of Ken's brother Steve, spoke to us at length about the business aspect of tournaments in the Youth Sports Industry. Paul also read parts of our manuscript and offered valuable feedback on adding facts to make our points even more vivid. Christina Vandenberg, a college level athlete and business developer, offered her insights on why and how she chose to develop the app called My Huddle, designed to address the critical emotional support needs of athletes in the Youth Sports Industry.

Thank you to our parents, siblings, and family members who spent countless hours supporting us and our children both on and off the field as fans and sage guides. We hope that sports will always be a special part of our shared lives together.

Preface

Millions of U.S. families spend tens of thousands of dollars each year to have their children participate in the Youth Sports Industry, which today is a $20 billion industry. It takes millions of families spending thousands—indeed, tens of thousands— annually for pay-to-play sports to generate that kind of revenue. Why should we care about how consumers of sports-related services and products spend their money? For one, because the costs associated with involving children in club sports are largely unaffordable to most families in virtually every organized sport that exists in the country.

Families spend their money on what is important to them. For example, many at all income levels participate in the $203.6 billion Disney industry by visiting the Magic Kingdom, watching its movies, and buying its merchandise. Some of these families can afford multiple trips to Disney each year with no strain on the family budget. Other families save for years to afford a trip to Disney. Still other families go to Disney when they really cannot afford to do so but happily go anyway.

So what is the difference between spending lots of money on Disney and spending lots of money on the Youth Sports Industry? The main difference is that the U.S. Youth Sports Industry, as it currently exists, may do more harm than good to many of its participants. For example, an epidemic of overuse injuries in youth athletes has resulted directly from this "professionalization" of youth sports.

The Youth Sports Industry, or YSI, has attached itself to virtually all youth sports. Those youth sports that have professional-level teams in the U.S. often involve the most numbers of club sports–level participants and the highest level of competition for the college-level NCAA scholarships. Soccer and basketball have been judged to be two of the most competitive and lucrative in the U.S. Youth Sports Industry today. Given Title IX laws, some college-level sports without national-level pro-team counterparts still offer college scholarships but struggle to find enough athletes to accept them. Many families in the know about the easier-to-attain scholarships demand that their child, whether interested or not, begin a sport like fencing or crew in order to access the port of entry into a select college or university. And smaller numbers of Youth Sports Industry professionals make their livings off of these families.

In this book, we outline the Youth Sports Industry's major problems. YSI accentuates the wealth and participation gap. Many children cannot pay enough to play, and those who do come primarily from families whose incomes are over $100,000 per year. One could argue that those who cannot afford to play at the club-sports level are the fortunate ones, given the ever-increasing levels of overuse injuries, the disempowerment of youth in an adult-driven industry, and much of the fun being removed from sports due to economic pressures the clubs face to win and the expected return on a high financial investment from the parent consumers. These club-sports-level-involved athletes no longer play simply for the sake of playing and the values they learn from the game. These youth have become valuable commodities to the parents who seek out this industry to land their child in the right college and to the sports clubs who secure greater earnings in a very lucrative industry if they play their business cards right.

Those youth athletes who cannot participate in the Youth Sports Industry find themselves shut out from a major port of entry into colleges and universities, given that college admissions at many select institutions are increasingly tied to participation at the club-sports level. In many sports, especially basketball, even ten years ago first-generation college students found their port of entry by earning a sports scholarship when their athletic talents were discovered. But today YSI is rapidly closing that door to would-be first-generation college-student athletes if they do not have the good fortune of coming from a wealthy family.

The Youth Sports Industry is a free-market system with no regulation, and unregulated industries lead to corruption. In proposing reasons to support regulation and reform of YSI, we hope to provide incentives to those key players who could create an important path to change—from parents to coaches to club directors to leaders in the medical field and health-insurance industries to legislators.

We explore who is making a living off of the Youth Sports Industry and who are its consumers. We explain a critical money-generating element of virtually all YSI clubs: the travel tournament. We provide a guide for wisely navigating this system should parents choose to involve their children in YSI. Finally, we explore what it might take to make critical changes in the Youth Sports Industry of today.

Our research to inform this book was multi-tiered. It included knowledge gained from our firsthand experiences as youth athletes and then as the parents of three youth athletes. We had conversations with dozens of coaches during our kids' sporting years. We spoke with dozens of team managers, parent volunteers who are often the most in the know about the inner workings of the sports organizations, and the coach employees. One team manager shared with us the content of her direct discussions with our local head of Oregon Youth Soccer. Our family has participated in coach-licensing clinics run by Oregon Youth Soccer, providing a glimpse into the complexity of training good coaches and the conflict involved when state-level sports-association leaders are paid by for-profit sports clubs.

When we committed to this book-writing project, we began more formal interviews of Oregon-based club-sports owners, directors, and coaches. We conducted extensive interviews with a national-level soccer tournament developer. We spoke with our local high-school athletic directors to learn their perspectives on the conflicts between local high-school sports and club-sports involvement in Oregon. We spoke with coaches from other states to understand the different laws regulating their local youth sports. We interviewed the head of an organization that brought leadership development through the game of soccer to different disadvantaged areas of the world and was thus a very helpful expert on how the scheme of youth soccer plays out differently on a global basis.

We interviewed a dedicated, ethical, local trainer for Oregon's Positive Coaching Alliance. We interviewed coaches at all levels in the youth-soccer arena including recreational soccer coaches, club-level soccer coaches, Olympic Development team coaches, and a former MLS Youth Academy coach. We had conversations with college-level coaches and heard many sordid tales from our children, extended family members, their teammates, and parents about college-level recruiting coaches and processes. We had conversations with athletes at the end of their youth-sports experiences, whether they finished their careers in middle school, high school, or post-college. We interviewed a former high-level college athlete who went on to create an app designed to help facilitate mental wellness for college-level athletes. We spoke to local sports doctors, surgeons, and physical therapists who pointed us in the direction of the need for this industry to address overuse injuries connected to yearlong, specialized youth sports.

We did a mass emailing to parents whose children had played on sports teams with ours throughout the past fifteen years, asking for their participation in filling out our survey about their family's experiences with the Youth Sports Industry. We asked for their consent to share their stories, good and bad, and their suggestions for reforms. In some cases, what we learned outside of this formal survey was observed from families along our years of sports parenting. These observations also served as stories of some of the extremes that can occur when the perceived stakes of these games are so high. We do not intend for the stories of these athletes, families, or coaches to be identifiable or to single out any individual as uniquely to blame for what we see as a complex system-wide problem. Each of the members who are involved in the Youth Sports Industry at so many different levels is influenced by, and has limited power to change, this highly entrenched system.

We also researched club sports–marketing trends on the websites of multiple nationally recognized, highly successful, and lucrative sports clubs from across the country. We examined the extensive research database, seminars, conferences, and policy-development platforms from the Aspen Institute's Project Play to guide our knowledge of the larger national-level trends occurring across all sports and age groups. We researched relevant academic literature in the fields of sports sociology, sports history, and sports medicine. We read many of the books designed for popular audiences that seek to spread the message of the ills of the trends in U.S. youth sports. We spoke to the published authors who knew that way too many kids were not having much fun in sports. Finally, we wrote this book to add our story to the mix.

Introduction

Our sports-life journey began together as a couple on the fields and pool deck of Ithaca High School in New York in 1983. It was clear that Ken was interested in dating Jean when he showed up at the door of her swim meet one day after soccer practice. It was clear that Jean was interested in dating Ken when she showed up at Ken's home soccer game one day just before swim practice.

We both come from large, active sports families, so we could find easy conversation about which team should be cheered for, the Yankees or the Red Sox. The American League East rivalry never got in the way of our early dating years, and Jean was even willing to go to Red Sox games once in a while when visiting Ken to watch him play a college soccer game in Boston. We had our clear favorites about which sports to watch and which teams and which athletes to cheer for.

For an Ithaca "townie" there was nothing like cheering for Cornell University when our local college ice hockey or lacrosse teams would compete for the national championship. Though tickets and a ride to watch Cornell's Big Red play could be hard to come by, we both have clear and fond early-childhood memories of listening to night games broadcast on our local radio station.

We were in the eighth grade when the U.S. Men's National Hockey team pulled off its stunning defeat of the Soviet team in the 1980 Winter Olympics in Lake Placid, and we both remember watching it on TV like it was yesterday. Ken has watched the movie *Miracle on Ice*, the inspiring true story of Herb Brooks, the coach of the 1980 men's Olympic hockey "miracle" team, dozens of times, and we have watched it with our kids almost as many times. Who does not get goosebumps when watching the grueling team selection, training scenes, inspiring speeches, and battle to win it all, against all odds? For us, and almost anyone we know, the story of *Miracle on Ice* captures just about all of what is great and worth fighting for to keep recreational, college, and Olympic-level sports alive and well for American youth.

We always saw sports as a positive and unifying factor in our lives, despite the painful yet standard losses for us, our friends, families, teammates, and our hero sports teams along the way. We had many friends who never played sports and many friends who did. In our high-school days, neither of us remember the possibility of playing sports in college ever having been an important topic of conversation among friends. We were there to enjoy our time in high school together.

A few of our friends went on to play sports in college, and we were happy for them. They were doing something they loved. We had met some of our closest friends on our school sports teams and made friends with a broad diversity of people despite the fact that, in those days, life circumstances and cultures would likely never have brought us together without being on the same sports teams. It was a time when sports still felt like the great unifier that it can be.

And yet, today, 25 years into our parenting journey, we wonder who is fighting to keep our country's youth sporting experience from being destroyed? We have seen in one short generation how much good and joy have been lost for our children when the sports experiences of our youth became a monstrous industry too big, greedy, and indifferent to stop devouring its youth athletes. We decided that together we would do our part in writing this book to join the fight that many authors, coaches, community leaders, medical professionals, and legislators before us have bravely led.

We felt it was our responsibility to protect the best that youth sports has always had to offer, just as we saw it change before our very eyes. It baffled us at many stages along the way—trying to figure out how to keep sports a positive experience for our family despite that nagging feeling that much of what we were experiencing with our kids was a cultural delusion. Despite our doggedly persistent and best optimistic efforts to see the benefits and opportunities for our children participating in the modern Youth Sports Industry, much to our dismay many of our experiences, when understood over time, ended up falling under the ugly, and horribly disappointing label, of a racket, plain and simple. As parents, we tried to bring the joy of sports to our children in the best ways we thought we knew how and always loved to watch them play. And yet, along the way, we gradually came to understand that some things had gone very wrong with youth sports and were rapidly getting worse.

Ken comes from a family of five boys who spent hours together in the backyard and on the neighborhood fields as kids, college kids, and grown men playing just about any sport one could imagine. Four played Division I soccer in college, and the other was a DI wrestler for a year. Thanks to a gifted group of teammates, Ken's college soccer team, in his junior year, went to the Final Four and finished the season undefeated, the penalty-kick loss in the national semifinal being officially recorded as a tie.

Jean comes from a family of four girls and three boys. The Linscotts played in varied levels of sports including competitive swimming, diving, ice hockey, basketball, baseball, softball, lacrosse, and crew. Some Linscotts played in the local recreational league only, some played in high school, some went on to play in college, and some are still playing as masters-level athletes and triathletes. One went on to make coaching her career.

In the 1960s, 1970s, 1980s, and early 1990s, all seven of the Linscott kids had the opportunity to play sports, despite our father needing to hold down two jobs to help raise a large family and to get us through college. No costly uniform packages, yearlong club fees, or air travel were required. Equipment was shared, handed down, purchased at the annual community sporting-goods exchange event, or put on our Christmas or birthday wish list as a special request. The same was true for all the Ruoff boys. Although we all likely dreamed at one point in our childhood of being a sports pro, and some of us did go on to compete in college and beyond, none of us ever felt pressure from our parents, coaches, or ourselves to keep playing one or any sport to secure a spot on a college team or the necessity of securing a college sports scholarship.

All seven Linscotts and all five Ruoffs went to college, secured good livings and vocations, and loved sports as fans and players, never having paid to play one day of a club sport. If one were to sit on the bleachers of a high-school or club sporting event in the 2020s, however, one might believe that only neglectful parents would allow their child to miss such a critical life opportunity as pay-to-play club sports.

Sports did not become a way for either one of us to make a living, though it has always been one of our shared joys. We chose separate professions that required doctoral-level education degrees. After earning his doctorate at Columbia University in New York, Ken embarked on an academic career as a professor of the history of modern Japan. Although he is not an expert on American history, the historian in him nonetheless sensed, as he tried to guide our children through the world of youth sports and eventually the transition to college soccer, that there had been unusually rapid change in this sector as a result of the emergence and development of the pay-to-play model.

Jean earned her doctorate in 1993 at St. John's University in New York in Clinical Child Psychology and has been practicing for 34 years. It is a profession that is unique in the breadth of training it provides in both what is normal for developing children and what can go very wrong. As a clinical psychologist, Jean has the privilege of having the time and confidentiality protections to understand deeply what is troubling children and their families.

One of the most important roles in daily professional practice is to help parents dispel myths about what common events in the life of a child are feared to be dangerous and what events may appear dangerous but are actually helpful to the child's longer-term accomplishment of independence, persistence, and emotional resilience. Any child psychologist understands how much time and creative effort it takes to dispel societal fear-based parental myths about what is emotionally harmful to children, such as the bubble-wrapping or helicopter-parenting approach to raising safe and healthy children.

And yet, the state of today's Youth Sports Industry we as parents have gradually come to understand in these past decades demands that we parent consumers who are in the know protect our children from an industry that refuses to do so because the child consumers are too young to protect themselves.

As we weaved our way through as parents and professionals, and unraveled the complex untruths in this web of fact omission at best and outright manipulation and deception at worst, we learned much that is wrong and dangerous about this industry. In hindsight, we wish we had done more to prevent harm to our children and their friends who were caught up in the money-, power-, and prestige-driven warping of youth sports that continues to run rampant today. We hope we can help prevent harm to others who learn from our personal stories and research.

Once trained to think like an academic, it is very hard not to see the world through that lens. Many families we have encountered in our children's youth-sports journeys have likely wondered how we as parents of nice athletic kids who have had great sports experiences and successes could be such killjoys and buzz saws and why would we not just go along or get along with the Youth Sports Industry. Sports are fun and positive after all, right? They knew that we too had played sports and were sports fans on many levels. So why could we not just be quiet?

What was going very wrong was not obvious to many eyes and neither was it to ours at first. But after countless hours over our three children's combined 48 years of sports participation discussing if, when, and how to support our kids' love of sports, when the financial and time commitment aspects of club sports would be barely affordable to us, we knew we had to approach this carefully. We also knew that much was not as it appeared, and it was very difficult to figure out why.

This book is our attempt to share with all adults who are choosing to involve their children in the Youth Sports Industry the insights we have learned along our personal, professional, and academic journeys. At the heart of our efforts, we hope to protect children and families and prevent further erosion of all the positives that youth sports can bring to athletes at all levels. We hope to sound the alarm once again, as has been done by previous authors who care about both youth and sports in the United States today. We want people to know that within the current largely unchecked, and somewhat hidden, power of the Youth Sports Industry, all is not well, and reforms are urgently needed.

Our three children's unique talents, passions, and personalities helped us to understand slowly, as we made it through game by game, and team by team of their sports years growing up, so much of what had changed from our youth-sports experiences as kids. At times, we desperately did not want to believe that these changes could be true. Using pseudonyms, we will share some of the stories that others have given us permission to share in this book. Some of our stories were based on observation, not direct interview. Each of their collective sports experiences include wonderful, happy memories of fun, effort, dedication, success, and good friends. Each of their stories also include great barriers and disillusionment, the types of which were almost nonexistent just one generation ago. Sports has always and will always involve disappointment, the "agony of defeat," and the feelings that come when you do not make the team. These emotions will always be an integral part of youth sports and in many ways are part of what makes sports great. You never know what the outcome will be, and the excitement and growth often comes in finding out, one game at a time.

Ken had the joy of coaching each of our children in their early youth recreational-league days. The Hobbits, Cheetahs, Mini-Pilots,

Elephant Stompers, and Labradoodles had some legendary soccer seasons. Carolyn, Megan, and Patrick can each tell you the score of the final match of the final game of the winning season and the winning tournaments from ages four through ten with Dad as one of their coaches.

It was not always easy and fun for the kids to have one of their coaches be their father, who loves to compete but hates to lose. But it is very clear to anyone who knows Ken that he also loves to have fun. Our best friends to this day still laugh out loud when they recall the words of Ken's speeches delivered to players and parents about how to be ready for a game and how to give it your all. We sat together in our living room and stole the chance any time there was a little free time left in the evening to talk about how best to help a kid on the team who was struggling with a certain physical, emotional, or behavioral challenge. We were a team as a couple who tried to help our kids and all the kids on the team have the best possible sports experience. None of the solutions we came up with were perfect or easy, but we knew the direction to set our compass.

The coaching, practice, and game-time commitment for a young couple with two jobs and three kids who all wanted to play multiple sports was enormous. But we never regretted those early investments of time, effort, and encouragement to help our young kids succeed in sports if they chose to. The newer and larger problem areas in youth sports only gradually became clear to us as our three children entered the club-sports system. The complex tale unfolded as we learned from child to child, year to year, sport to sport, and when we began to ask ourselves and others some tough questions.

Each of our children is a passionate athlete and has been so from a very young age. The kids were given the opportunity to be in great physical shape, and we will never forget moments when all you could see as a fan was their clear love for the game. They competed at all different levels, with many successes and championship seasons. As a family we flew to Texas and watched the University of Portland Women Pilot's soccer team, with Megan Rapinoe and Christine

Sinclair, go on to win a national championship. Our kids learned sportsmanship and leadership, each taking their turns as team captains along the way. They were recruited for college sports. They have great memories of some of their coaches, teams, and teammates and all the grueling work, goofy antics, fun, and heartbreak that come with being a part of something larger than you, a member of a team. And they experienced a truckload of bad memories, bad experiences, and bad coaches too. We only hope that the good outweighed the bad, and that their sports journeys were positive enough to pass on the good that was learned along the way to the next generation. We learn perhaps as much if not more from our bad experiences, one might say. But if we learn, we try to minimize and correct that which leads to bad experiences. We believe that our children will have a whole lot of corrections to make to right the ship for the next generation of youth athletes. But they can't make these changes single-handedly.

Coaches loved to have Carolyn, Megan, and Patrick on their teams, and some quite often made a big public fuss about their talents. But from as early as age ten, when each began participating in club soccer, their attempts to be a multisport athlete and a kid, not a pro, who kept having fun playing on teams with their neighborhood and school friends, were met with coaches' intense displeasure. This story would go on to repeat itself again and again. The dilemma was simple: Playing a club sport year-round meant it would often overlap or conflict with other "in-season" school or recreational level sports. The game of "punish or permit" attempting to be a multisport athlete while also playing a yearlong club sport had begun, and no parent, kid, or coach quite knew what to do about the situation.

We began to notice that our children had very mixed feelings about playing amid this conflict. It was a system-wide problem that had no clear or simple solution. It was a system-wide problem that plagued youth athletes across the country and resulted in medically unadvised single-sport specialization, overuse injuries, unnecessary coach pressuring tactics and scorn, and a whole lot less fun than we had playing sports growing up. It was a system that led to many days of our children coming home in fury or tears about what they were experiencing on the practice and game fields.

We hope that all of you who have been a part of the sports journey with our family who read this book will understand the best of intentions we have in telling these stories. We hope to illuminate for many future sports parents with athletes of all levels of ability the pitfalls we experienced along the way. We hope that the knowledge gained from this family's experience will help guide the decisions that are right for your family and your children in their unique sports journeys.

Chapter 1

Who Are the Consumers?

Who **participates in the Youth Sports Industry,** and why do they choose to do so? In this chapter, we explore the families and the reasons they have for participating: the good, the bad, and the ugly. But it is equally important to ask, Who is not participating, and why are they not taking part?

Initial Reasons to Play

It may start with the simplest and purest of intentions. Playing on a competitive sports team can be a good way for kids to get exercise, make friends, and learn the value of teamwork. Parents can make new friends, share parenting resources, and enjoy the fun of cheering on their children and the team. The children and parents can feel a part of something bigger than themselves, a team of which they can be proud. These are noble goals for any sports team, no matter the cost.

Many parents, when asked, will state that the main reason they pay to have their child participate in pay-to-play sports is that their child greatly enjoys the experience and can learn valuable life lessons by being a participant. Both the parents and child may enjoy the relative prestige that comes with being able to associate with an "elite" youth athletic organization. Parents may love sharing with their friends and neighbors that their child is traveling around the country with a high-achieving sports team, retelling tales of the most recent nail-biting, amazing win, or commiserating about the most recent heartbreaking loss. We all love a good story.

Parents and children alike enjoy their "sports weekend vacations" in which all can enjoy time spent with teammates and fellow parents cheering on their children, watching a game that many love or have come to love.

But what can start as normal, if expensive, reasons to participate in pay-to-play sports can evolve over time. As a child advances in age, parents, athletes, coaches, and club directors can lose sight of the most important reasons that children thrive from participation in sports. Parents who are overinvolved in setting and realizing the goal of prestigious athletic and academic outcomes for their children are contributing to serious emotional and physical injuries in their children. Coaches whose ability to earn a living depends on their youth teams' successes are contributing to serious physical and emotional injuries in their athletes and serious financial distress for the players' families. The adults are taking the fun out of youth sports for their children by taking them far too seriously and blindly overinvesting in winning. Buying success is very different from earning success.

Different Ports of Entry and Stoppage

Examples of entry and stoppage into the Youth Sports Industry tend to focus on youth-club soccer, but with some slight differences in the timing, cost, and duration of the seasons they could just as easily apply to youth hockey, baseball, volleyball, lacrosse, water polo, fencing, and many other pay-to-play sports teams. So how do children and their families end up in the world of pay-to-play? Children can come into the pay-to-play soccer system from several different avenues. They are enticed to begin as young as preschool age in pay-to-play soccer classes, such as one in Portland named Little Kickers. They may also enter youth recreational soccer in kindergarten-age-group divisions such as Kick and Chase. Or they may enter into the Junior Academy divisions of club-soccer teams.

In the case of Little Kickers, the highly structured soccer classes for preschoolers and their parents are run by coaches who are employed by or own the Little Kickers franchise. The paid coaches are often kind, talented, attentive, energetic, and loved by the preschoolers they teach. Many know a good amount about both soccer and children and are trying to eke out an honest living in an industry filled with many other earnest and hopeful coaches attempting to do the same. Parents are participants from the beginning with their little kicker, out on the field guiding their preschooler through the drills to facilitate group management for the coaches and to keep the child attentive and engaged in the drill.

It is a teaching model that is very popular and works well, so what is the problem? The preschool training classes can be the first foot in the door of the parent being overinvolved and overinvested financially in their child's sports participation and progress. It is the first example of a "spot"—a head start that is paid for, not earned.

Is it fun and important for parents to spend time playing with their child, especially doing shared activities that they both enjoy, or sharing in the child's sports passion? Sure. But since when does a family need to pay to facilitate parents' ability to play sports with their child? Might children's athletic development still happen if they were left to play soccer with friends and siblings in the backyard, with parents occasionally glancing from the kitchen window or jumping in for a few passes from Mom or Dad during a break from mowing the lawn? Might the results of child-driven participation be better for the children than the current model in which the children eventually come to be the laborers in the multibillion-dollar industry their "play" supports?

Most children and parents love their experiences with Little Kickers and, if they have the time and the money, are happy to sign up for more. It is a way to get out of the house, be around other parents, get their child to expend some energy, and start the family early on its path into youth sports. If a friend's athletic son or daughter was getting better and better at soccer skills at age 3, would you wait for your equally athletic child to tell you they want to join? Or would you wait for your preschool-aged child to express independent interest in soccer at the risk of "delaying too long" or "falling behind"?

Thousands of parents across the country ask themselves similar questions every day. What is the possible payoff for starting early is almost always asked, but what is the cost of not waiting for the child's lead is almost never asked. Educators have longstanding disagreements and ever-changing curricula regarding when and how to begin teaching reading to a child. Yet within the current state of the American Youth Sports Industry, with almost no regulation or enforceable standards, it has become commonly accepted and largely unquestioned that earlier and more is better when it comes to engaging youth in sports training.

Some programs such as Start Smart Sports, developed by the National Alliance for Youth Sports and sponsored by its corporate partners, have attempted to begin healthy sports-culture-environment training for parents and their preschoolers. They have developed Start Smart programs for soccer, football, basketball, tennis, lacrosse, golf, and basketball. Participating teams and leagues are provided with basic equipment, coaching manuals, videos on being a good sports parent, and a parent-child workbook to set a healthy tone from the beginning. However, as is the case with many organizations designed to help rectify the wrongs in the Youth Sports Industry, these are voluntary programs not mandated by governing sports bodies in the United States.

The next door of entry in soccer is through the local recreational youth-sports programs. In the case of soccer, this program level is popularly known as "rec soccer." Some clubs call the first year of soccer Kick and Chase because it appropriately describes the form of soccer "played" and at which most kids have a blast. And they should have fun, if the goals of the program remain age appropriate and child focused. These programs are typically affiliated with the state soccer association and charge a modest registration fee. As of 2020, recreational soccer fees rarely exceeded $100 per season. Additionally, there are often arrangements that can be made with the league to have the registration fees covered by scholarships or waived in the case of children whose families cannot afford to cover the cost. The goal is inclusion, not exclusion.

The coaches are all volunteer parents who in the majority of cases have one or more of their children participating on these teams with their neighborhood friends. For example, in one of Oregon Youth Soccer's recreational clubs, Mt. Tabor Soccer, children can play in local neighborhood leagues with reasonable fees and parent volunteer coaches until about the fifth grade. These days though, very few children and families who are serious about athletics participate at all or for long in the recreational-club league. Although the financial expense is designed to be affordable for all, and the level of competition is highly variable from team to team, admittedly even these recreational leagues are no strangers to ill-behaved parents who see it as their job to scream "Kick the ball!" from their lawn chairs. This is true in spite of sincere efforts by the recreational clubs to enforce basic behavioral standards.

At the end of the fourth- or fifth-grade recreational-soccer season, a turning point is reached. Most of the players who would like to play at a more competitive (i.e., prestigious) level will try out for a pay-to-play soccer club. Most clubs will be happy to take the parents' money, regardless of whether or not this level of play, time commitment, or the child's physical capabilities and interests are a good match for a club's program. They have their numbers to meet in order to pay their staff and coaches, as well as to field teams, not all of which are competitive. More players, more teams, more club fees paid, more salaries earned.

It would be a false assumption that the transition to pay-to-play immediately results in a better group of players or a higher-quality team. From personal experience, our daughter's first competitive-level team, a club U-10 team, would have been soundly beaten by her local neighborhood recreational team. This example also provides a window into who is being left out, for only two girls from her recreational team transitioned to club soccer. That being said, at the older ages, there is generally no comparison between skilled club teams and their recreational counterparts.

The fallout effect of many of the more competitive and financially able players leaving the local league is significant. Those who are "left behind" playing at the recreational level now have a different composition of teammates. If you are a parent with a child who has even a somewhat strong interest in and love of soccer or another sport, at this point the game your child loves has likely changed dramatically at the recreational level. Meanwhile, there is a better but drastically more expensive game available at the competitive club level that most will not want to miss, especially since it is year-round (it takes time for parents to realize simply through experience that more is not necessarily better). The pay-to-play option also provides for fun and prestigious travel opportunities—something kids hear about from their older peers and want for themselves.

The parents are left with a dilemma. Choice one: Stay at the less competitive, recreational level, thus conserving invaluable family time not to mention financial resources. But keeping children in a recreational-level experience means their chances of developing into a better player suddenly become slim. This leaves them wondering why they cannot play on a better soccer team when so many friends who "aren't even as good as me" are leaving to play on a club team. Choice two: Switch to a competitive, high-cost club where children will not "miss out" on their (or their parents') soccer dreams and futures. A complicating factor is that players who stay and are "too good" may have to contend with the undercurrent of parents and teammates still playing at the recreational level quietly wondering, "Why are those kids still here playing so seriously?"

An additional path of entry is to start in the Junior or Youth Academies of the competitive-soccer programs offered from the earliest ages. There are different versions of tryouts for these programs, but for many there are no cuts until the older age groups. For a price of around $1,000 per year, a child can have a professionally coached soccer experience from age 5 on, complete with often three or more nonparent coaches who are paid to guide the child to continue developing his or her highest soccer potential.

If your young child becomes interested in finding a club team to join when the recreational single season has ended but the club team is mid-year in its yearlong season, a parent who makes an inquiry call to the prospective club coach might receive an interesting question. "Is your child big?" None of our children were more than average height at any stage of their growth. Two of our children were physically late bloomers. All of them were very talented athletes in their own ways. This question might have been a good clue that the coach wanted to know if this parent had a child who could help the team of 10-year-olds win more games in mid-season right now, using a size advantage that would not be sufficient to serve the team well in only a few short years. Rather than trying to learn about the child's character, interest, current skill level, and love of the game, it was about whether it was worth the coach's effort to add a new kid onto the team within the club's short-sighted plans rather than long-term development. The coach would have had to contend with unhappy parents, mortified that this child did not try out with the rest of them. A walk-on, mid-season player could be a dreaded threat to their precious and closely monitored (via parent stopwatch) child's playing time. There would also be plenty more kids showing up for next year's tryouts, so why bother with taking in a talented and dedicated yet smallish 10-year-old player when a full paying team was already in place.

The competitive clubs are often fewer in number and in more distant locations than the youth recreational leagues. So joining a pay-to-play club will likely mean far more time spent traveling, typically by car, for training and games, as well as far less money in the family budget for anything but participation in a specific sport. A five-minute walk or drive to the neighborhood park can easily get replaced with a 100-minute round trip across town in traffic. Most 5-year-olds might much rather spend that extra time playing at home, which has its own value and also does not as a rule contribute to the risk of an overuse injury. How kids spend time tends to inform the parents whether or not it is the child driving the interest in the sport or if the sport is being delivered on a silver platter to the child, who is not apt to decline. Kids who love a sport will find a way to practice it.

In terms of soccer development, the child's car time might be better spent kicking the soccer ball around in the backyard, developing natural abilities and love of the sport in fun and creative ways. In addition, many families do not have a parent available to start the long drive during work hours to get the child to club practice on time. One of many peculiarities of the world of pay-to-play is that it pays next to no attention to realities such as that many parents must work set hours, which makes the demands of family participation in pay-to-play highly burdensome (multiple weekday practices at distant locations), not to mention that children are supposed to attend school (not take time off traveling to and from tournaments).

The driving- and workday-interruption demands were barely manageable for us, and we were two working professionals with jobs where we could mostly set our own hours. When we entered the world of club soccer, it was very often the case that one of us had to pick up the kids directly from school at 3:00 and make the fifteen-mile drive to practice, hoping traffic would cooperate to allow our oldest to arrive for a 3:30 practice on time. Other seasons it was a twenty-mile drive through the most heavily trafficked areas of Portland during rush hour to arrive for a 5:30 or 6:00 start time. The younger children, ages 7 and 3 at the time, had to ride along. But by age 5, the younger two had their own extracurriculars. So we had to hope that the other teams practiced at a similar time and location when the other parent could not get home from work on time to watch or drive them. There were at least five years when all three needed to be at different fields for different teams, often for practices that occurred at the same time. Carpools were necessary for survival for two-parent working families like ours, and if your precarious two-person-carpool teammate stopped playing on the team, there was a mad scramble. Occasionally some coaches had the nerve to attempt to shame the child in front of the team, demanding to know why they were late. Last we knew, no 10-year-olds have ever had any control over their school dismissal hour, the traffic conditions, their siblings' practice schedules, or their parents' work schedules.

But the competitive arms race is not geared toward all American families because for most families participation in pay-to-play is a fantasy. Rather it is geared to the elite. If we do not arm our child with sports weapons, someone else's child is already developing his or her arsenal and we will fall behind, reasons the elite family, which has the time and resources for such musings. So start the kids now, no matter the cost, no matter the impact, and, often, no matter the interest on the part of the child in the sport. The quest for prestige is everything to some, so the goal is to avoid falling behind (or maybe even getting ahead) because otherwise your 5-year-old might get cut from the elite team next year!

A former college teammate told us that his son spent most of his teenage years living in fear of being cut from the Seattle Sounders Academy Team, afraid to ever miss a single event so as not to give the coaches an excuse to release him. This academy's schedule can easily include five practices a week and two or more games per weekend, often out of town. Travel for games is frequent and extensive. There are no acceptable reasons for missing a practice, including holidays, required school events, or family weddings, and of course never a reason such as wanting to attend a friend's 12th-birthday party. If practice has been scheduled, you will be there or risk losing your spot on the team. Your childhood is owned by the Academy before it has hardly even begun.

Once in the competitive system, the time and cost commitment to both the children and their families is great and becomes progressively greater as they get into high school. Looking back, it was not uncommon for families to describe the experience as if they had gotten caught in a whirlpool that swirled them around and around to higher and higher levels of commitment in terms of time and money. Families with a high school–aged state-level club player in the Portland area will pay approximately $1,600 per year for basic fees, not including the costs of uniforms, tournament fees, and travel. A family with an Elite Clubs National League–level high school–aged soccer player might pay a $2,300 base fee but easily could pay $10,000 or more annually in travel costs.

For older age groups in youth sports, the so-called training fees actually represent not much more than a few drops in the bucket of costs incurred mostly by extraordinary travel costs. The costs in terms of time are also significant, so much so that pay-to-play should unquestionably be thought of as a lifestyle choice. In order to meet the relentless team-training and travel demands, often three or more practices a week and two or more games most weekends, the list of what the club-level child athlete may sacrifice has grown quite long. On an Oregon-based ECNL soccer team for girls, four practices a week are routinely required at the high school–age level, and the entry age for this league can now reach down to 11 for Junior or pre-ECNL. Not much if any time is left for family dinners, family vacations, going to movies or parties with friends, joining other high-school clubs or sports teams, or just spending leisurely time at home.

To imagine what a high-school student's schedule might look like if he or she attempted to play both a club sport and a high-school sport, here is an example of what one of our daughters' high-school weekdays looked like for several years. Our children all attended a very academically demanding college-preparatory private school, so the academic workload was substantial. School: 8 a.m.–3 p.m., school basketball practice: 4:15 p.m.–6:15 p.m., home to change and eat: 6:30 p.m.–7 p.m., soccer practice: 7:30 p.m.–9 p.m. Earliest time home to start homework not finished at school: 9:30 p.m. Or during lacrosse season, lacrosse practice and eat in car: 3:30 p.m.–5:30 p.m., soccer practice 6 p.m.–7:30 p.m. Homework done and in bed: often midnight or later. Where is the time to rest your mind and body, have time to yourself, or just do nothing for even a few minutes?

There are other levels of youth competitive soccer as well, including the U.S. professional men's and women's soccer-academy teams for multiple age groups. There are residential schools, both domestic and international, that recruit and train young promising athletes, some of whom may go on to play at national or Olympic levels. Some of these young athletes may move out of state or out of the country, spend countless hours of training and family funds, with family and peer-group time sacrificed, only to end up dropping out of soccer before high school. There are players—far too many—who develop overuse injuries or suffer soccer-related impact injuries and who no longer can play the game again. What is simultaneously odd and alarming is that this model of specialized, intensive training is coming to include, at least in the United States as a result of the Youth Sports Industry, so many young athletes who will never even play in college not to mention at a higher level because of injuries.

Most pay-to-play sports models, at least by the time the child reaches the age of 12, are prohibitively expensive for the majority of American families and are thereby exclusive. They tend to be structured far more around the goals of the adults who organize, earn a living off of, or pay for the sports rather than the children who participate in them. For many children they are not fun for very long. By age 13, 70 percent of youth in the U.S. have ended their participation in organized sports.[1]

One cannot have a sports team without willing, able, and available players. A space to play and something that resembled a soccer ball was all that was previously necessary for kids worldwide to play soccer, and in much of the world it remains all that is necessary. The same was true for nerf football, stickball, pickup basketball, and so many other activities organized by the kids themselves. Forty years ago, if a kid stepped outside on any given weekday after school, rain or shine, that child could round up some buddies to play. No parents, coach, referees, rides, schedule, contracts, uniforms, or costly equipment were needed. If a child was to play in an organized recreational-sports league one generation ago, all that was needed was a minimal registration fee. The coaches were volunteers.

One of our daughters' most fun soccer experiences came at the college-student age when the global pandemic, against all odds, forced most college-aged and youth athletes' relentless structured schedules to come to a screeching halt. For many of these college athletes it was the first time since they were age 5 or younger that they were not participating in an organized sport that ruled their daily lives. After a novel eight-week trial of online learning beginning in March of 2020, when the pandemic shut college campuses and their sports teams down, she decided that online learning for the fall semester of 2020 was not what she considered to be a viable college experience, so she took a leave of absence. With much effort, trial and error, and persistence, she put together a travel experience that, among many other adventures, allowed her to play soccer with newfound friends in Belize. Their "organizing strategy" when they wanted to play was to ride to their friends' homes on bikes and golf carts to round up any available players by whistling from the street to their balconies. Hey, time to play! The pandemic was keeping most students and workers worldwide out of their normal daily routines, and so, as a young adult, she finally got to play soccer freely. Round up the neighborhood friends who were always there and always up for playing a pickup game, head to the beach, and play soccer in the sand till the sun sets and you could see the ball no longer. The goals were made from a palm tree and a water jug, or two water jugs filled with sand. Repeat the next day. Fast friendships, formal and informal, were forged among international athletes who played simply for the love of the game. It was a time and sports experience she and her friends will never forget. Two of her closest friends anywhere in the world now she played with on the beaches of Belize. They played for days on end until she could not even walk anymore one day but it was too much fun to stop.

On her next travel adventure that pandemic year, in Kenya, during a study-abroad term, her favorite memories included playing soccer informally on the beach where anyone and everyone could join in. They made goals from sticks. Whoever had a ball would bring it, and rides were offered to the beach by passing motorcycle drivers who saw her soccer ball in hand. The soccer ball was a sign for all nearby to pitch in however they could to help make the game happen. Many fast friends were made in Kenya too with the beautiful game on the beach connecting these soccer lovers.

Consider post-pandemic times in the U.S. If kids can even find an open grassy space to play that is not already in use, the field often has a sign saying "sanctioned play only" or a locked fence making it clear it is not open for child-driven games. Fields are reserved for youth leagues or clubs who pay, in Portland, a minimum of $125 per hour ($150 if they have lights) to rent the coveted field space, if they in fact can find any field space available to their organization. Today, one can see hundreds of youth out playing sports on any spring, summer, or fall day in the greater Portland metropolitan area, on school fields and city-park fields. During weekends of the winter months, school gyms and specialized indoor facilities are filled with team after youth team playing from early morning into the late evening. It might appear that youth sports are thriving based on the number of fields, not only outdoor but also indoor, and how often they are filled with players and parents alike. But what one is seeing is mostly pay-to-play sports.

What easily-accessible fitness and sport opportunities are available today to the children whose families cannot afford the cost of pay-to-play sports? We estimate that the cost of a typical pay-to-play club sport would easily eliminate accessibility to 80 percent of American families, with the relative sacrifice required of the families who do participate increasing dramatically as one moves away from the upper 10 percent.

As Hope Solo, former U.S. Women's Soccer National Team goalkeeper, so aptly put it: "Soccer right now has become a rich white-kid sport." By Solo's account, her family would not have been able to afford to let her play soccer if she were a youth starting the sport today.[2] The gutted budgets of public parks and recreational facilities across the country make access to recreational youth sports, once free or affordable to all, increasingly a relic of the past that elicits nostalgia in those old enough to remember previous models. Obesity-prevalence rates in American youth are currently estimated at an alarming 18.5 percent, which is in part connected to the lack of affordable sports and recreational opportunities.[3] We cannot afford to ignore the fitness needs of the vast majority of our country's youth.

The Overinvolvement Disease

What is occurring on the fields and sidelines for the athletes participating in this generation of youth sports is of critical importance to their development. If the linking of youth sports to college education is uniquely American, so too is the widespread linking of dysfunctional family dynamics with the excesses of parental overinvolvement in the Youth Sports Industry.

Problematic family dynamics exist worldwide and will continue to exist throughout time. These dysfunctional dynamics across generations in most countries have involved chores, sibling rivalry, family loyalty, responsibilities for a family business, the caretaking of family elders, and degrees of allowable autonomy, among others. Dysfunctional family dynamics are also related in some countries to academic success and also sports achievements. Parents will always be tempted to condemn their child's performance when speaking to their child while at the same time brag about or inflate their child's performance to other adults.

The extraordinary excesses of money that are involved in the U.S. Youth Sports Industry and its perceived link to college and prestige present a new catalyst for highly dysfunctional family dynamics. This new dysfunctional driver is stunningly powerful and in many cases dangerous to the health of a family. If coaches can lose their livelihood without generating winning teams, and parents can adopt the viewpoint that their financial investment in their child's sports career requires a return on investment in the form of prestigious-college entry, scholarship, or fame, it's easy to see how the proper priorities for coaching and parenting youth can become obscured. The coaches are paid by the parents, who pay to make a child into a form of success that accounts for a minuscule percentage of cases.

A common sideline drama in the Youth Sports Industry is hearing angry, misguided parents berating, overinstructing, and shaming their players' every move at every competition and every practice. Many parents have come to see this outrageous behavior as normal, responsible guidance for a child of athletic promise. They worry that if they don't engage in it their child will fall behind.

We know of one well-meaning but overinvolved father who was infamously banned from multiple fields and asked to leave multiple clubs due to his incessant and brutal berating of his daughter, the referees, or the other teams. His daughter withstood the spectacle and went on to play a few years of college soccer before her career ended early with too many concussions.

The children are equipped to look and act like mini pros, complete with high-cost uniforms (often with sponsor logos included on them) and salaried coaches. Perhaps this contributes to the high expectations from their paying parents, who might easily be confused for their child's hypercritical workplace micromanager instead of their most supportive fans. And if you watch the children closely, their stress level while playing a "fun" activity is striking. Many pressured kids and teens look nervously for approval before and after executing a play, which they may execute haltingly with anxious avoidance.

They cry, they tantrum, and may leave the game mid-play because the perceived pressure can be too much. There are numerous "pride injuries" per game, performed by those children who have learned to act and speak the terms of being physically injured when in fact feigning physical injury after having made a mistake is nothing more than an attempt to save face and preserve pride. Or their purpose may also be to preserve the pride of their parents, who are frightened for their child's team standing and are loath to admit that their 10-year old might have just made a plain, old-fashioned mistake while learning the game. Mini pros are not expected to be learning, they are expected to know already.

Our family recalls two tween-aged pride-injury pros, who we will call Carter and Maggie. When the team started to get behind in a game, and the parents' nerves started to rise on the sideline, one could predict, almost like clockwork, when the injury would happen, but rarely could anyone figure out what exactly had happened to Carter. Carter would head to the ER with a parent and return to school with some headline of rest and restriction, which would last for a few days. Then the details of what it was, and when Carter was able to return, would change and blur in people's memories, and soon enough the scary, mysterious, and vague injury was no more or forgotten. When Carter's teammates were older and began to tire of these mysterious dramas, if he was challenged regarding its veracity or it was reviewed on the ever-present youth video footage and the facts did not align with the tale, Carter's parents would soon let others hear about it and smoothly suggest that in fact the doubting teammate or parent was being negligent about the doubting child's own body and injury-safety judgment.

Maggie, the 10-year-old club-soccer player had a nickname of "Maggie Flopper," and even her own teammates would sigh when the game was stopped for the fourth, fifth, sixth, seventh time due to Maggie's dramatic fall and siren call of tears and alarm. But after every disruption of the game, up she would pop again, and the game would resume after the latest stop. We are hard pressed to recall a close foul or even the threat of a possible strategic foul from the opposing team ever being connected to Maggie's flops. We suspect it was rarely much fun for Carter or Maggie to get through these games. Face-saving pride injuries can be exhausting to keep up with for the child, the parents, the coaches, the referees, the opponents, and their teammates.

How to get a child to cooperate happily with going to their required organized youth-sports practice has become a common, urgent concern among parents who bring their child in for consultations with child clinical or sports psychologists. Before arriving to the field, even for practice let alone the amplified version on the stage of an actual game, parents contend with child reports of sudden stomachaches, panic attacks, mysterious aches and pains, tantrums, refusals to get ready, claims of too much homework, and a myriad of symptoms of competition stress. The adult-driven culture of shine and win at all costs inherent in the design of today's Youth Sports Industry serves very few children well. When there are competing parent-guidance truths, in other words work hard, get better, and keep your commitment to the team versus find an activity that you love and pursue that to its fullest, it is a rare parent who can leave the decision of what interests the child up to the child. The stakes for many parents of allowing their children to decide what they want and what is fun for them have come to appear too high, far beyond the stakes of success on the field one Saturday for 9-year-old competitors. Who is driving the train?

Some children can thrive and cope easily under the relative stress of competition. They greatly enjoy the privilege of playing at a high competition level from kindergarten through college and learn valuable life lessons along the way. For other children, adults' overinvolvement in driving the child's agenda—to psych them up, train them up, and keep them "in the game " no matter what—can do far more emotional and physical harm than good. And when it is not fun, the children will quit. In the best-case scenario they quit and go on to enjoy another activity, inside or outside of the sports world. In the more harmful scenario, these children become largely inactive or have no other alternative activities or adult-supported interests that can be easily accessed, leaving them at risk of obesity, juvenile crimes, and substance abuse, among other problems.

One tragic worst-case scenario involved a former teammate of our son's. Gerod began missing school, missing practices, and getting in trouble, lots of trouble. No one could reign him in, or perhaps some adults connected to his life, who might have had some influence, did not try what decades of history have often shown to work: firm, consistent rules and expectations. The story from one perspective goes that his soccer coaches hoped they could "save him" by heaping high praise, leveling no consequences, and starting him in every game, regardless of Gerod's missing months of practices and the rest of the off-field chaos that was unfolding in his life. He had also been purported to be one of the team's best players of promise. But Gerod never learned life lessons through soccer as the club founder would have wanted. Soccer did not keep him out of trouble when there were no contingencies being enforced for the privilege of participation. If you come to practice, keep your grades up, and stay out of trouble with the law, you play. If you can't meet those standards, despite your talent and "promise" in soccer, you don't play until you can fix those things, perhaps even with the support of your coaches and teammates. Instead, he ended up as a juvenile delinquent with an alcohol problem who committed a violent felony. Were they actually thinking that giving him carte blanche on the soccer team would "save" him, or were they primarily thinking that winning was the first priority so put him on the field, regardless? Were these young male high school–aged club-soccer players viewed as commodities primarily instead of as individual young men in need of firm guidance and mentoring through the game of soccer?

Perhaps at equal or worse risk than quitting are the children who learn to disconnect and simply go through the motions, serving the ego needs of countless misguided parents and coaches through unwanted and unnecessary hours of "playing" the sport. They hesitate to let go of the current and future prestige prize, so hallowed by their parents and peers, and the attention that being an athlete brings them in their family and social circle, even when they have grown to hate the game. How could they take away the part of their identity that means so much to their parents and peers by quitting the sport? They stay to play because many feel like they have to, not because they want to.

One telling tale was told to us by a long-term, highly respected club-soccer coach and former member of the early version of the Portland Timbers as well as the Canadian national team. A group of middle school–aged girls he coached hid away from the field in the Liberty High School cafeteria for weeks after arriving at practice in order to avoid doing mandatory team-fitness training. The elaborate scheme started with the girls being dropped off at practice on time by their parents but skillfully avoiding any coach's awareness that they had arrived. Once fitness was over, they showed up at the field and hid the fact that they had been dropped off for practice on time. Their web of deceit finally unraveled when the parents confronted the coach about their child's playing time and the coach connected the limited playing time to the missed fitness training. At older ages, when the girls could drive themselves to practice, they may have just not shown up—until the coaches and parents began to talk. Many of the players may passively show up and simply go through the motions, despite the great cost to themselves, their relationships with their parents, their coaches, their identity development, and often to their teammates. They become essentially zombie teammates who are well-veiled drains on team morale.

In the case of youth-club soccer, the specialization of sport happens often far too early and long before the child has had exposure to other sports, organized or informal. The same is increasingly true of the position played by a child in any given sport. It is all too common for a youth-soccer player to be identified by his pay-to-play coach as, for example, a "left defender" at, say, age 10. With every game seen as a must-win match, he or she is never played in another position by the coach. Before long, both the parents and the player accept the notion that the young player is a specialist in one position and resist opportunities to play elsewhere on the field, should they ever be given that opportunity (many are not in light of the pressures to win).

But this is no way to teach the game of soccer, nor the game of life, to a child. And the results of this odd early specialization are all too apparent. If one witnesses a position change during a game, it is not uncommon for the young athlete to crumble due to the fear that the athlete does not know how to play a new position and as a result will be penalized by coaches and parents for playing poorly. The adult message sent between the lines to the child is: Don't take risks or try anything new unless the adults involved are guaranteed a win or a good performance outcome. But these are short-term strategies for winning, not long-term strategies for developing the player and the individual.

Stepping back, it is utterly ridiculous to conclude that at the U-11 level the necessity of winning is so great that, heaven forbid, the left back be given an opportunity to play forward, thus opening his or her eyes to the game from the perspective of a forward, with various positive outcomes. It is possible that the so-called left back is actually a fabulous forward. It is also possible that with an understanding of the game from the perspective of a forward gained from experience at that position, the player ends up being a better left back. Perhaps most importantly (but largely forgotten), maybe it would be just plain fun for the youth to have a whirl at playing forward. But the short-term need to win often trumps all else.

A very small percentage of youth are served well by the American Youth Sports Industry. Those who are served well may be very blessed to have been gifted with athletic talents, a certain body type, and a temperament that thrives on the competitive demands of sports from a very young age. They may also have the luck of thoughtful, emotionally mature, and financially well-off parents. They may land in a well-run club with well-trained coaches where guidelines and priorities are developed and carried out with purpose, research, and ethical principles as primary guideposts. Yet this healthy combination of children, parents, coaches, and clubs seems to be far more the exception than the rule. The old and easily accessible solution to building healthy, strong bodies; providing fun social activities; and learning important life lessons through playing sports, organized or informal, continues to exist only in withered form. It has been replaced by the current model of pay-to-play youth sports that is creating more problems than it is solving.

Prior to the Youth Sports Industry, children from just one generation ago got started in their favorite sports in the following ways: Kids from any income level would play sports on any playground or sandlot or field or street or backyard. If they did not have the right equipment, they would improvise. Almost no one had fancy uniforms that designated affiliation with a prestigious club. No one needed them. Today, does it not seem more than a little ridiculous that the families of young kids must fork over $350 or more for fancy uniform kits that are required in the world of pay-to-play. This certainly does not result in a higher level of performance than if they were outfitted in

T-shirts and shorts that were more or less the same color. Even on our daughters' school basketball team, for years the families were required to buy expensive basketball shoes so the team could all match. The coaches explained to the girls that they had to "look good to play good." Kids previously played on their own together far more often than is the case today, including kids from a greater socioeconomic range. They played in their free time and played because they loved it. Some with great talent combined with a passion for a game persisted, worked hard at it, and came to excel greatly at their sport at an organized level. They learned how to earn their spot, play for their team, win and lose.

This is how many a high-school, college, or professional player from around the world got started only 40 or so years ago. But today participation in sports often needs to be purchased from a club team. Parents a generation ago had far fewer irrational fears about the imagined "skyrocketing risks" of their child being able to play outdoors in parks on their own. They had far fewer fears of the "high-stakes risks" of letting a child decide what sport or activity they were passionate about and how seriously or how long they pursued it. So, just one generation ago, if a kid wanted to go play sports, all they had to do was step outside and find some friends. In this generation, even a child who has permission from caretakers and is interested in going to play pickup sports in a park on their own could have a hard time finding peers who are free to join and a place to play.

Have there always been parents, who for good or for bad reasons, became overinvested in their child's sports training and development? Certainly. But what is new is the lack of many other viable alternatives to pay-to-play in youth sports and the extreme cost to play as the child advances up the age ladder in the Youth Sports Industry. Nonetheless, colleges provide preferential admission and even scholarships to these privileged athletes, many of whom are chosen from a tiny socioeconomic slice of the United States.

Not enough youth currently have opportunities to stay physically active and socially engaged with their peers in a way that does not overly rely on sedentary socializing in, for example, the synchronous video-game format. However, the video-game industry has a clear corner on the kid-sustained interest market. The gaming industry pays attention to what kids like: free exploration, on their own terms, or together with other peers of their choosing.[4] As opposed to the sports parents who are frantically trying to get their kids to play the adult-directed game more and better, gaming parents are at a loss as to how to get their kids to stop playing. Perhaps the reasons are more complex than simply the fearful lament of the "addictive nature" of video games, which so many parents love to invoke and invoked in generations past about paperback novels and other newly feared vices. Kids may love video games so much because almost all parents are at a loss to dictate anything about how the game should be played. In other words, video games are popular precisely because they constitute a parent-free zone.

The tried-and-true benefits of regular fun exercise, teamwork, and team membership through organized-sports participation open to all economic backgrounds have been sidelined in the United States. In addition, parents who have invested incredibly large sums of money in their child's athletic development can come to possess a dangerously entitled sense that they are owed a return on their investment, leading to devastating levels of parental overinvolvement in the child's sports experience.

How might one of the authors, a clinical psychologist with over thirty years of experience in working with children and families, best briefly define parental overinvolvement in a book on youth sports? This is a daunting task to put in writing what can take hours, weeks, and months of face-to-face, individualized clinical work with families to understand what overinvolvement means and then to help them see themselves in the mirror. Perhaps one of the simplest ways to define an overinvolved parent is one who insists on controlling the uncontrollable for their child while blindly or ambivalently denying and ignoring the emotional and physical costs to the child, the family, and the parent-child relationship. In the world of youth sports, a parent cannot control either a child's temperament, physical talents, or development rate, nor the competition, the coach's decisions, or the referee's decisions.

The parents' overinvolvement, rather than constructive guidance, leads them to push their children beyond their physical and emotional limits. They push their children until it hurts and to a point that is often beyond repair. The parents may hide from club coaches or on college-athlete recruiting profiles the actual number of concussions their youth player has sustained to prevent an early ending to the child's sports career. One family who did just this, and the fact that they shared with others that they would not take their son to see a doctor because if he were diagnosed with a concussion he would not be able to play, put various parents in an ethical quandary about whether or not they should intervene for the sake of the child. It has become commonplace to see and hear overinvolved parents consult and compete with one another regarding their strategies to pay, deceive, manipulate, repair, demand, berate, or bribe everyone involved in the Youth Sports Industry to control the uncontrollable. Concrete examples of overinvolvement range from screaming at or assaulting referees to hinting at the possibility of moving to another club if playing time at the child's favorite position is not increased.

Overinvolved parents are often the very same parents, ironically enough, who have conscientiously read numerous parenting books. They have attended countless parent-school outreach workshops and parent-team meetings run by teachers, counselors, coaches, and consultants, all aimed at fostering healthy parent-child relationships at home and school and on the sports field. These same well-intended, zealous parents typically conclude that the overinvolved parents are some other kid's parents. They view themselves as the responsible, well-informed, well-positioned parents, poised and ready to enhance every possible opportunity for their child's success no matter the cost or time commitment to their child or family. And this earns them their parental high-status stripes in the eyes of many. Any box to check off on the list of "responsible, involved parents," they are on it, and they will pay for it. Why would they risk letting their child miss out, lose out, or get behind?

But the consequences of unintentional and alarmingly common parental overinvolvement are harmful. Doing too much for your child can be just as bad as, or worse at times than, doing too little. Why do millions of parents require their children at younger and younger ages to participate in activities that are leading to astonishing levels of overuse injuries and surgeries that require months of physical and mental rehabilitation to allow their child the possibility of just being regularly physically active once again?[5] The American Academy of Pediatrics warns of skyrocketing rates of soccer-related emergency-room visits. Between the years of 1990 and 2014, it recorded a rise in the annual rate of soccer-related injuries at 111.4 percent and a rise in the annual rate of soccer-related concussions of 1,595.6 for every 10,000 soccer players during that time period.[6] Behaviors that are popular among many well-to-do parents may still be considered symptoms of a serious disease. Sadly, what has become the normative definition in the elite-youth-sports world of what "responsible" parents do matches all too well the definition of harmful overinvolvement.

The old child-driven participation model has been replaced by an inequitable, exclusive pay-to-play model fueled by the dreams and fears of parents desperate for prestige, blinded by the illusionary hook of potential fame, and hovering to guarantee their child's success, even if the price is their child's physical and mental health. If there exists a "golden ticket" for purchase, the "best" private trainer, the most elite summer camp, the most technologically advanced speed and agility training, the most successful mental-game coach, many will desperately seek to buy it. The success of the Youth Sports Industry clubs so often revolves around selling the dream with a strong dose of fear about missing out on the dream mixed into the sales pitch and proving to parents that their program is superior to the rest and will put their child on the fast track to elite success. Yet, the vast majority of children end up quitting youth sports by the age of 13, even if they did have the means to access an organized, pay-to-play experience. The ever-rising obesity and mental-health problems[7] in American youth, both those who are served and underserved by the youth-sports system, scream to us as parents and professionals an obvious truth. The emperor in the Youth Sports Industry has no clothes. There is something seriously wrong with this system.

Parents Know Best Impact

And yet, this the club-soccer experience has become and remains the coveted gem for many families who will stop at nothing to maintain a child's spot on a team, influence their child's playing time, and get their child ahead of teammates. This "parental steering" is often delivered to a child without exploring what the child wants because the parents will "always know better" and do not want the immature or short-sighted child to miss out on "all future options."

Countless parents become blinded to what highly experienced and respected coaches, physical therapists, physicians, and mental-health experts believe to be in the child's best interests. The parent decides that he or she must stop at nothing to facilitate the child's quest for the holy grail of a college scholarship, Olympic dreams, professional soccer stardom, and fame. Or maybe even if none of those lofty goals sought by so many and gained by so few are reached, parents are more than satisfied to simply maintain bragging rights—"my kid plays on a travel soccer team that is going to San Diego this weekend for a tournament." Parents' appetite for prestige by proxy may be likened to drug abuse with its short-term highs, complete with all the lies and manipulations that addicts desperately use to keep their sources coming. With the investment of countless hours and thousands of dollars into their child's sport, it is hard to imagine there is much time left for parents to foster a sense of self-worth in their child.

In our years of parenting our children through competitive soccer to date, and still going, we can say with great confidence that truth is stranger than fiction when it comes to what we have seen. Granted, parents behaving badly were certainly easy to find in our generation's experience in youth sports that was more youth driven and characterized by coaches who were typically volunteers. But remember the "return on investment" model? What parents pay entitles them to many "privileges" never before assumed by parents in regard to how they communicate, often trespassing boundaries that formerly would have been considered firm with players, other families, coaches, and referees alike.

Just when we think we have heard the worst yet, there is another story about out-of-control parents who believe they can fully control outcomes, competing against one another to top all others. One family we know has a 16-year old adolescent, Sam, who is a solid player but not currently a starter on his high-school team as of the sophomore season, when we started writing this book. He was working with an independent trainer, doing supplemental independent training sessions with the club coach, working with a motivational trainer, doing independent early morning workouts at the parents' work facility, and working with a college-sports-recruiting specialist, all in addition to three or more weekly club practices and often two games per weekend. These young, privileged athletes who have had every imaginable form of training handed to them have come to be known in some of the college-coaching vernacular as the "overserved athletes." They are known to suffer from burnout before even stepping foot onto a college athletic field.

These overserved athlete's parents might arrange Sam's social schedule for him, both for good and bad reasons. They might invite a teammate, Danny, from an economically disadvantaged family, if that teammate is considered the best on the team, to stay with them for days on end at their luxurious family home. The goal is to increase the chances that the economically poor but talented Danny will "like" their son Sam on the field and therefore pass the ball more often to him. More passes from the best player, Danny, may increase Sam's chances of making a better showing on the field, at least in the minds of overinvolved parents if not coaches who understand the game.

But what does Sam want? Can he choose his friends at age 16? What if Sam is not onboard with his parents' plan to market him, their player-son? Who is the player here, and who gets to make the final decisions if there is disagreement between the parents' plan and the son's plan? Is this an effort to control the uncontrollable, or is this a savvy and kind sports parent? The parents share with other parents that they are trying to make a difference in Danny's life, who is not only poor but also surrounded by several dysfunctional family members.

In the minds of some, time for Danny spent with a "good family" will surely make a difference to the team, and they are of course good team parents. The parents' welcoming generosity is believed and lauded by most, while some of the motives for doing so remain hidden. The desire to get one's child in good with the alpha player or alpha group member is certainly not new. But the depth of overinvolvement, the price tag, and the costs to the child that goes with this parental maneuvering is now more striking than ever. As it turned out, during the summer between Sam's junior and senior year of high school, his parents moved him to another club after his club coach committed two unforgivable sins. First, he left him off the top team for the State Cup competition. Second, he gave his honest appraisal that the kid was not qualified to play Division 1 college soccer.

We knew a family with a 12-year old, academically challenged daughter, Cece, who woke up at 5 every morning to go work out with weights at the fitness club before school and who by 14 had developed back injuries and her first of several ACL tears. No coach or trainer had recommended this extra weight training and brutal daily schedule for Cece's growing preteen body. Cece was already a respected, well-liked starter on the team who was seen as doing just fine at the club level, so why the need for extra? If Cece had an independent thought opposing that punishing schedule, it likely may have been quickly brushed aside by parents who knew what she needed and were just being very good parents who supported her dreams.

Consider also the experience of 14-year-old boys who are participating on the local Portland professional soccer club's prestigious youth-academy team. Given that this is a program sponsored by the region's professional men's soccer team, the costs are primarily covered by the professional organization. So this could be a rare bargain for parents in the Youth Sports Industry if their child is good enough, or connected enough, to make the team.

The Timbers Youth Academy has daily practices that can easily run two and a half hours and sometimes end late on school nights without a stitch of advance notice. In this "development" system, boys may practice with these prestigious teams but are not guaranteed any amount of playing time in games. Those parents desperate to keep their golden boy on the team and get him some minutes will stop at no behavior or expense to get what is wanted.

This includes the common practice of paying for supplemental training sessions with an academy coach. The academy coach, paid barely a living wage for full-time coaching, wants to earn more money and so offers (or does not discourage if some other private trainer is doing the training) hope. If the young player just does more training, at 5 a.m. every day before school, perhaps this could lead to more playing time. Work more and harder is assumed to be best, consequences and impact steadily denied. Why? Because there is no easy way out of this desperate system for many once they have gone down the rabbit hole and once it becomes clear that the elusive goal of becoming a pro soccer player may not be within the youth athlete's reach.

A parent whose son was a participant in the Timbers professional youth-academy-club system said, "Soccer [today] is like quicksand—you don't know you are sinking in it until it is too late." The Timbers should know better.

To do what is reasonable, affordable, healthy, and in line with a child's physical- and emotional-developmental needs is estranged from what the Youth Sports Industry beast needs to stay alive. The more families that buy into the "mini pro" model, the better. If the children are being treated and trained in line with a pro system, they must really be that good, reason the parents.

Arguments have been made in other books about the dangerous excesses in training in the U.S. youth baseball system[8] that these children, whose growth plates are still developing, are being asked to train more than what would be considered safe for their pro counterparts. The USA Gymnastics association for decades has struggled to right the wrongs of the career- and life-ending physical injuries and equally life-threatening emotional toll that these training models and intertwined abuses have exacted on young Olympic-level and Olympic-hopeful female gymnasts.[9]

We sadly recount an all-too-vivid, common, and close-to-home story told to us by close family friends about their wonderful son Jacob and one miserable weekend of his club-soccer experience as a high-school freshman. It was a rainy, just-above-freezing Saturday in a typical Portland November—the time of year that most club teams are revving up to judge or show their prowess as the local contender to be reckoned with or to justify why parents are spending thousands of dollars to send their children traveling multiple times all around the country. The team had been placed in at least three different local-, regional-, and national-competition leagues, and the schedule in the months ahead would be relentless and punishing on many levels.

On this miserable day, which started for the players at 6 a.m. or earlier to arrive at warmups for their first game, the team had already been scheduled to play two league-based competitions. Even one game at the intensity level of high school–aged boys-club soccer is physically demanding and risky in these types of weather and field conditions. Yet two of these games per day has come to be seen as normal, especially over a tournament weekend. But on this particular Saturday, with two league games already to play, the coach had scheduled a third game for these boys. It was to be a friendly game with a local girls-club team, announced to these boy players and their families at the last minute. The arrangement was likely to facilitate a club-to-club alliance in the making or to please a coaching colleague in a way that would help someone climbing the coaching ladder. In other words, it had absolutely nothing to do with the young players.

The players were exhausted, wet, cold, and hungry and at a field that was miles away from their home neighborhoods, where they might have gathered dry clothes and a quick meal. Those players who had the nerve to decline the coach's mandate for a third game of the day were derided for their shaky commitment level and mental softness. The parents, most of whom immediately saw the absurdity of this schedule, were in a desperate, lose-lose dilemma once they heard the coach's demands. To go against the coach was to put their child's position and standing on the team in jeopardy.

And so, despite her son Jacob's imploring that he not be required to play the third game, our friend Jesse did not inform the coach that her son would not be available for that third game. Jesse's decision to put her child in an unnecessarily physically risky position, not to mention advocating for the coach's unreasonable decision over her son's reasonable decision, still haunts her today. Jesse, who by most accounts from all who know her, is considered to be a wonderful, firm, and loving parent, finds it hard to fathom that she was actually the one who decided to require this of her son. However, Jesse finds herself in very good company—including that of the authors—of strong, caring, well-meaning parents whose stomachs turn when in hindsight they look back at some of the terrible parenting decisions they made while trying not to drown in the quicksand of the Youth Sports Industry.

A more standard example of overinvolvement is the parents who come early and stay late before and after every one of their child's practices, from age 5 on, in the hope of "running into" the coach and thus hopefully scoring some points for their child. It is not unusual for coaches to depart quickly from practices and games, following routes designed to avoid parents, but overinvolved parents stalk them mercilessly. On one Olympic Development Program team of U-16 boys, many of whom can drive themselves to practice, the majority of parents still come to watch every practice. As they do with their club-team events, parents scope out the coaches' entrance and exit paths in order to "casually" fit in their daily player checkup and political-maneuvering conversation. Some insist they must ask about every angle and every detail of every decision the coach has made about the day's practice and all decisions being made in the future. Is there a sign that my child might be falling behind teammates' level of play? If so, how to fix that, wonder the parents. Organize the next team party, complete with a nice gift for the coach?

One local club team has had some recent successes winning at the state and national level. The parents have come to believe that this team is exceptional with a capital E and therefore that each of its team members by definition is and must continue to be exceptional—a dangerous recipe. Some of the less affluent families will give up their own house and home and go into debt in order to keep attending the "essential development experiences" for their child to play out of state four or more times per year with this exceptional team.

If they decline to travel with the team, all worry, what will happen to their child's spot and standing on the team? The team is vaunted to their local fellow club-soccer parents as exceptional, a means to justify the travel to continue their player's development. And then, when the team is upset locally at a state-level competition, the parental shame and confusion is so thick no knife could come close to cutting it.

The players shame their families by losing in the State Cup? Wow! What message is being transmitted to the young boys on this team from their parents' viewpoint and behavior? If having fun, getting a little bit better each year, and learning life lessons through sports were still the answers for most clubs' and parents' team cultures, we would not be writing this book.

The Prestige of It All

In a short time the apple does not fall far from the tree in terms of kids mimicking parental behavior. How can it be that before 12-year-old middle-school children have even thought about what they will be studying in high school and how they want their high-school experience to turn out that they are frequently bragging to their athlete, and nonathlete classmates, who may be less economically advantaged or less in the know about the braggart's charade, about their participation on a travel club team?

The lies start out small but grow larger. Younger kids brag that they will be attending an out-of-state tournament in which they are a top recruit for several elite-college-level coaches. In rare cases, it is possible that this seventh-grade child has such talent that coaches nationwide already want to see him play and ask him to verbally commit to their college. But in most cases, the children whose families are paying to attend showcase tournaments are no more athletically talented than their classmates.

Their children, as young as middle-school aged, have become self-promoters and self-publicity hounds. As of 2017, Joey Erace, famously known as Joey Baseball, a 10-year old baseball prodigy in the making, had 24,000 Instagram followers and millions of other kids scrambling to become Instagram influencers in turn.[10] A local high-school sophomore, Danny, from an underprivileged family, used his own money to pay for a video of his league soccer game to be made and posted on SSVisual Works Instagram film.

While refereeing, our college-graduate daughter met a 15-year-old girl who was also refereeing the same game. The teen shamelessly tried to dupe her elder, a former ECNL alum, and any nearby younger peer who could hear her loud boast that her participation on an ECNL girls soccer team was "basically the U.S. national team." It's not. It's just another team.

We have met several middle schoolers and high schoolers who have told tales including that they were top Stanford University athlete recruits. (Their "evidence" of being a "recruit" might include one mass email sent to all Oregon Youth Soccer high school–aged athletes from the coaches who were trying to fill their college ID camps with thousands of paying customers that summer). Currently in the women's college-soccer world, Stanford is often ranked in the top 10 in the nation, a team which might easily be able to choose from the country's Junior National Team to help fill its annual recruiting class.

One high-school freshman, Brianna, kept her well-crafted tale of being a top, national-level, "committed" recruit going for at least three years. Many adults in the local-school and soccer community were instructed by Brianna's mother that coaches and trainers in the state knew Brianna already had the "full package" as a player, she just needed to work on her "swagger." This in the face of a reality that suggested she was a player of large physical stature who was a solid average player, even for a very small high school. When Brianna played, she had some impact in some of the games, but one would never guess that she could be a player who stood out at the national level.

Our children, who were raised to be independent thinkers and taught to have the courage to exercise their right to speak their minds, dared to suggest to peers that Brianna's boastful tale seemed unlikely. Our children, who still grounded their beliefs in demonstrable facts and merit, were soundly chastised by Brianna's other spin-doctoring peers. These "politically savvy" peers would not see or say that the empress and her entourage had no clothes and firmly labeled our children as being "just jealous!" Though the word-of-mouth and social-media ruse lasted for years, and many believed it, eventually when the hype had settled, for some unknown or unexplained reason, Brianna did not actually "commit" to the nationally ranked school after all. The ending of the glorious recruitment tale went quiet. We do not know if Brianna ever went on to play soccer in college, is still playing soccer, or has any interest in playing soccer. In small communities it is often easy to find this out, but it has never been mentioned again to those who suspected all along it was likely a great tale.

Imagine the pressure this young woman must have felt to impress and her dilemma about how to live with the reality of her athletic present and future situation. Would it not have been simpler, emotionally healthier, and more fun to be able to live in the present of who she was as a player versus who the story said she needed to be? The Youth Sports Industry is complicit in many of these unnecessary tales of deception and struggle.

The real ending to the story was not at all part of the master plan. Fiction can create realities for some well-connected self-promoters. Witness the Operation Varsity Blues crimes and the still legal but ethically compromised admissions tales that open the doors to college admissions and sports-team membership for those athletes who appear to be meritorious, even if simply by social-media legend and a hefty parental donation.

But for as long as people would listen and believe, the shameless self-promoter had some unknowing adults in the community crowing that this average-level female athlete "would play for the U.S. National Team some day!" Brianna, even as a freshman, promoted the image that she was too good to need to play with her high-school team and did not want to risk injury playing with a lesser level of competition, yet she often showed up and practiced by herself on the sidelines when her high-school team practiced. Brianna, who had no other apparent conflicting commitment, given that she was right there doing her own "special" training on the sidelines of a high-school practice, was only playing with her lowly high-school team when she felt up to it. Sham-enabling friends and families connected to the team were trained to cheer wildly when she chose to grace the team on game day with her amazingness and worry when she did not show up. How could the team possibly function without her? And yet, if another equally or more talented and dedicated player on Brianna's team was publicly acknowledged with a Player of the Game award, there were thousands of rationalizations to repair the wobbly moment that the myth was publicly in question. Why would the team coaches tolerate this behavior from Brianna and her family? Well, there might be losing at risk for a decidedly average high-school soccer team. Maybe they purposefully chose to just ignore Brianna's behavior, or even more likely tried to help her do the right thing. But Brianna could not stop participating in her own family "culture of greatness" story.

Worse perhaps than the lies is the obvious impact that this club-sports culture of "show myself off to get noticed" has on how poorly many of these children behave as teammates. We have repeatedly watched egregious player refusals to make the obvious and best pass to a teammate to help the team win the game when an individual fears giving up the personal opportunity to shine. She holds the ball too long and inevitably loses the ball. Those less versed in team play at a high level in the sport marvel at the selfish player's ball-hogging skills and ignore the turnover result. Sadly, there currently exist many "I"s in "team."

We have heard stories of coaches who keep certain competitors apart in matches because they have been known to purposefully attempt to hurt each other. We have read that it is a common practice for athletes to be advised against sharing where they are being recruited for college sports with their fellow club teammates. Why? It has apparently also become common practice for teammates, or their parents, to contact the admissions offices at universities with sordid tales of why the college should not be admitting this athlete or that teammate of terrible character and should really be admitting their child.

So why tournaments? Parents and players go because the tournament is there, it can be fun, the family can pay, the child has practiced many hours, and it is good for parent and player bragging rights. Tournaments abound in spades across the United States for youth-sports teams because tournament organizers can gross fantastic profits over a single weekend. Curiously enough, in many youth sports, and especially in baseball and basketball, there are numerous "national championship tournaments," plurality in an area where the wording suggests singularity. But if one's child's team has participated in or even won such a tournament, why should parents and players get bogged down in the details, why let the truth get in the way of a good story? The prestige earned may be in direct correlation with the profit made, and so tournament organizers and families can come to have a symbiotic relationship.

Some parents are courted by foreign coaches who have come to the United States to bring players whose wealthy families are willing to pay to attend their home country's soccer schools. Parents send their children away and pay hefty tuition, room, and board fees for an international soccer-based school, at times as early as middle school. We often hear of their unremarkable or miserable attendance and early return home. Yet perhaps living away from home and training in another state or on another continent will be the box that needs to be checked off to control the prestigious outcome. Despite the athlete's average talent level at best for many of these high-price-tag-paying families, the mantra is spare no cost. But spare the emotional and physical costs? Are the injuries connected to the athletic program that these parents have so carefully crafted for their child? That is a very unpleasant topic for most parents to face.

Other parents help plan, organize, and/or fund-raise for the team to attend an international tournament to a country where the coach would like to travel. The parents reason that this could be a potentially critical learning experience, though costly, and great college résumé-building material. Sadly, very, very few 13-year-olds' families can afford the time and money this type of sports-related travel-experience requires, even if the child does have a talent comparable to the ones who travel and play far and wide.

Given a coach's desire to make the team's sports participation be the international trip's top priority, the players may sit in a hotel room during most of their international experience in between games. Some parents pull their hair out about what to do if the team is going and they can not afford the cost: What will happen to their child's standing on the team? Others from the same team on the higher end of the socioeconomic ladder are asked to consider funding the costs of one or more teammates who cannot afford it. Despite the fact that many very wealthy parents can afford these costs, after years of living in quicksand they come to question the benefits of agreeing to pay for such things. Is it really spare no cost?

In most cases, claims by clubs that fund-raising will make a tangible difference are a joke. The time and effort it takes for these already-incredibly time-stretched club-sports families to organize and fund-raise might allow for approximately $100 or so per player to be raised every year, despite the best of intentions. In other words, with much time and effort, they might raise a drop in the bucket of the actual fees and travel costs of pay-to-play. When implored to fund-raise, more-experienced parents with means immediately write a check to avoid being sucked into fund-raising schemes that return less than if a parent simply worked extra hours at a minimum-wage job and contributed his or her salary.

Keep Our "Little Stars" Playing

Perhaps for a few years parents believe they should spare no cost. These are "prestige war" times, and these times require wartime measures. All is fair in love and war, is it not? The parent "loves" the image of their prestigious mini pro, and the coach alternates between being an opponent, often when the coach is doing no more than being honest about a player's strengths and weaknesses, and an ally, when the coach is seeing the situation correctly. Compliment the coach, take him or her out for a drink, offer tickets to the local pro team's next game in the best front-row box seats available, let the coach have a weekend at the family's vacation home; ideally, make the coach downright dependent on you. Or scream at the coach, spread stories and rumors, organize the team to leave the club for a more prestigious coach (or a coach more open and bendable to parental influence), defy the coach's recommendations, undermine what he or she says and does, and spread rumors about your child's more successful teammates. All is fair in love and war in the Youth Sports Industry for all too many parents.

The *New Oxford American Dictionary* defines the word "enmesh" as follows: to cause to become entangled in something. It is a family-systems-therapy term frequently used to describe a very problematic family dynamic in need of correcting. Simply put, parents and coaches in many teams across the world are terribly enmeshed, and the consequences to their children are being seen far and wide. The children and the parents need the coaches and clubs for their players to gain higher-level athletic-prowess exposure. The coaches and clubs need the parents to pay, and to keep parents staying and paying, the clubs need teams that win, at least a few games, to provide bait for buying the dream. One cannot extract the paid coaches from the teams or from the clubs who need the parents to pay and to pay in so many unnecessary ways.

Mental-health professionals have written for decades about the widely understood negative impacts of parental overinvolvement on children's mental health. The Youth Sports Industry includes the over-involvement of not only parents but also often coaches, trainers, consultants, and other sports industry–related adults. It has become far too easy in this Youth Sports Industry for the benefits to the involved adults to outweigh the consequences to the child. While adults involved in YSI can easily rationalize that more of the child's year-round sport is better for the child, in reality this equation is mainly in the interest of the myriad layers of entangled adults and often inflicts more harm than good on the children involved.

The self-guided youth athlete, more common of one generation ago and much harder to find in this present generation, plays because he or she loves the game, it is fun, and he or she finds great meaning and purpose in the challenge of excelling at sport. The child learns positive lessons applicable to most any aspect of life in the present and future. The child decides for himself or herself, with the guidance of other adults, at what level and for how long he or she would like to play a sport.[11] Some of the greatest emotional challenges to the self-guided athlete are simply learning to gracefully accept one's own physical limitations, endure the heartbreak of losing, and develop a new identity when one's playing years have come to a close.

The other-driven youth athlete, prodded along by prestige-seeking parents and peers, college-athlete recruiting services, clubs and coaches who must win to earn and succeed, is at high risk for negative impacts. The youth is at risk for mental-health disorders and alarming levels of overuse injuries, at risk for eating disorders, at risk for suicide. The child burns out at a young age from a sport, though many adults involved in the child's sports life refuse to acknowledge burnout or address it when it is clearly present. The child struggles to make independent decisions, relies on or silently resents the adults who tell him or her when to get up, what to eat, give reminders of the daily practice regimen and game schedule, pack the bags and decide how much effort and enjoyment to dedicate to the sport.

Some student athletes have been personally told by overinvolved college coaches that there are only certain, less time-consuming academic majors that will be allowed if they are to play on the college-sports team and keep their scholarship. A coach telling a player what major or career they can and cannot pursue in college? How could this not be seen as immediate grounds for firing? And yet for many parents and coaches, this has come to be accepted as normal and necessary for "scholar-athletes." How can a coach's guidance be seen as normal when most of these college students are young female and male athletes for whom there exists no hope of being paid a penny to make a living playing their sport beyond college?

Alarming numbers of young athletes experience serious mental-health challenges.[12] Anxiety and depressive disorders are reported to university student-counseling centers at levels unheard of just a decade ago. Both student athletes and nonathletes alike comprise students seeking mental-health services on campus. However, compared to other students, student athletes experience extra stressors associated with academic performance given the daily practice, game, and travel-time demands; pressure to perform to maintain their position on the team; and the physical stress demanded of their bodies to compete at a college-sports level.

In an article in *Atlantic* magazine, the squash coach at Harvard University was quoted as saying he currently had three athletes on his team for whom the coaching staff does mental-health safety checks three times a day.[13] This degree of mental-health challenge for athletes is no longer seen as unusual by the coaches who steer these teams. An internet-based service named My Huddle (www.joinmyhuddle.com) was developed to serve the unique mental, social, and emotional needs of today's high-school and college athletes. My Huddle offers student athletes text-based coaching regarding mental athletic performance, stress management, college-sports-recruiting stresses, and emotional support during the injury-recovery process.

These other-driven athletes have watched for years the model of parents who will stop at no behavior or cost to ensure a spot for their child on a team or at a college. The lesson of earning your position has often escaped them, even in the arena of sports. If enough playing time or a starting position is not occurring, by default many youth athletes, like their parents, presume the reason and the solution lies within everyone else's hands. What will this example encourage for these students when they enter the work world?

How many overinvolved parents value their children's autonomy to create their own solutions for earning their own spot on a team or admission to a college? How many overinvolved parents recognize when a child is ready to hang up the uniform and try a new pursuit in life? The answer, unfortunately, is very few. These athletes have observed many coaches and parents model the lesson that a winning, prestigious outcome excuses any wrongs and harms done along the way to obtain it. Or at the very least, the damage done to the youth on the path to winning most often has been deflected to the responsibility of others to solve, denied as being a serious ethical problem when it is at least legally allowed or ignored in terms of its broader impact on our society as a whole.

The collateral physical, mental, and financial-health damage wrought by many parents and clubs/coaches who profess to believe that this system as it exists is normal, good, and necessary for all players' developing interests is ignored. It is the bottom line of profit in the Youth Sports Industry for those who make their living from it and live off of parents and players desperate for prestige, many of whom have no insight into, and have avoided reflecting, upon their motivations.

Why Do They Still Keep Paying?

If parents had any idea how coaches talk about their player-children to other coaches, pointing out their deficiencies in the sport and how a place on a college team is a fantasy even as they accept the annual fees, they might end the "buy the dream" payments sooner. But coaches need paying families to make a living, so why puncture the dream? The families will finally learn when college coaches take no more interest in their sons and daughters other than encouraging attendance in an ID camp. The bubble of the chased college-sports-team spot, or preferential admission to the prestigious university of their choice, slowly and painfully begins to burst when the ID-camp slog begins. One group of college ID-camp coaches after another happily takes hundreds of families' camp-attendance fees and may end up recruiting none of the participants. Or, they hold the bait out for longer, stating to the athlete, "We would like to see you play more." Translation: Coaches would like you to pay for attending more of their ID camps or find a way to attend another showcase that the coach might be attending but the athlete's team might not be attending. But far more often than not the player is briefly told the coaches are not interested and do not have a spot for the player on the team. More likely, the player is given no additional feedback at all after having heard a faint promise of a playing possibility from the college ID-camp coaches.

Why do families consume the Youth Sports Industry's products at such an astounding cost? As more is written in the media, more books directed at parents are published, and more word of mouth is passed down from within parent communities about the incredible costs and impact of such an industry, what keeps it alive and thriving? How long will it last in its present form?

There is some speculation based on declining numbers of players at the high-school club-soccer level, and on declining numbers of youth-soccer participants in the United States overall, that a change may be on the horizon for the Youth Sports Industry.[14] There are other youth sports where the numbers of participants are still on the rise, suggesting it may just be that the participants are switching from one pay-to-play sport to another. Some parents remark that specific niche-sports college-recruiting markets may have become saturated, as in too many players searching for too few spots, and that the crazed quest for scholarships will end.

Other indicators suggest that if the hopeful students choose the "right sport" in their high-school years, such as women's rowing or men's fencing, their chances of finding a team and a scholarship are higher.[15] Judging from the number of online college-bound athlete-recruiting businesses and the thousands of individuals they employ and the profits raked in by national organizing bodies, it appears that the Youth Sports Industry is still alive and well.

Yet after all the youth's time, stress, injury, and enormous financial cost to families, remember, only roughly 7 percent of all high-school athletes go on to play college sports.[16]

Chapter 2

The Pay-to-Play Youth Sports Market: The Providers

The Clubs, Leagues, and the Importance of Branding: Elite with a Capital E

There are so many actors in the youth-sports market these days, so many who are making a living from youth sports that one wonders where to begin. Let's start with the pay-to-play sports clubs and elite leagues. The clubs and leagues bring together a triangle of actors who substantially shape pay-to-play youth sports, namely club administrators, entrepreneurs, and sportswear companies. It is only natural that travel agencies, for example, have developed packages to cater to YSI, for which travel to tournaments is fundamental. But the travel agencies do not directly impact the development of young bodies and minds so they have no responsibility in this area.

It is the pay-to-play youth-sports clubs that are on the front lines and bear the most responsibility. Although more and more clubs and leagues are registering themselves as Limited Liability Corporations or S Corporations, initially many of these clubs and elite leagues registered themselves as 501(c)(3) nonprofits for the purpose of taxes, which may seem ironic considering that they operate very much like businesses. But the nonprofit sector in the United States is massive, and many tend to be administered similar to businesses. They tend to compete, often fiercely, with other nonprofits in the same sector. It would be mistaken to think that individuals working for 501(c)(3) organizations are paid minimally because of the organization's non-profit status. In fact, sometimes employees are paid handsomely. The entire nonprofit sector deserves a rethink in terms of which organizations should qualify for tax-free status, but that is a topic for an entirely different book.

The websites of pay-to-play sports clubs inform us about their culture and also about their marketing strategies, which often have strong commercial overtones. Each club does offer youth something that can be deeply meaningful, namely the chance to pursue a sport, to be part of a soccer, volleyball, basketball, lacrosse, baseball, softball, or hockey team, among others. There are regular practices and games. In some cases, there also may be a significant social component.

These activities keep youth focused on something that, if administered correctly, can be a facilitator for positive growth. Involving youth in sports and other activities is by now a time-tested strategy for keeping kids, especially as they reach their teenage years, out of troublesome temptations. There are positive aspects to pay-to-play sports because sports can impart many life lessons. Like other group activities, they play an important role in socialization. The bond between team members can be strong, incredibly strong at times, providing a community for participants. In a basic sense, the role of pay-to-play sports overlaps with the role that organized youth sports have been fulfilling ever since they developed. But at the same time, sports, similar to social media, are neither inherently good nor bad. Rather, it is how sports are carried out that gives them positive or negative meaning or some combination of positive and negative.

There are some notable differences between pay-to-play sports clubs and the recreational youth-sports programs that are withering away. Having one's child participate in pay-to-play sports is no longer a question of responding to an "all welcome" sign followed by filling out a simple form and paying a nominal registration fee. This was the case with recreational youth sports up until the 1980s and remains true for those recreational programs that still do exist. In going down the path of pay-to-play sports, parents initially pay a small tryout fee, typically equivalent to the registration fee for recreational sports that covers the costs of the entire season. What follows in pay-to-play sports, however, is a large fee for the basic services, regular practices with a "professional" coach, and regular local games officiated by paid referees. Almost all clubs either make the family pay for the entire season upfront or sign some sort of promissory note committing them to the full season's player fees. Parents typically must also commit to pay even greater sums to underwrite travel to tournaments, especially as the player advances to older age groups.

Unsurprisingly, many parents want to know what they are getting in return for such a significant investment of resources. The simple fact that parents look upon their kids' participation in a pay-to-play sport as an "investment" that requires "return" evidences how much has changed in just one generation. There are many areas where a club must "brand" itself to be successful in the youth-sports "market." There is considerable consistency across the various sports in terms of what is viewed as making a club successful. With the dominance of the internet, clubs concentrate on putting their best foot forward on their websites and through social-media posts. These websites provide a snapshot of the culture of pay-to-play sports.

First, rankings matter. Rankings do not refer to a club's overall standing in the community. They do not refer to the fact that local notables commend and recommend a local youth-sports club for having consistently helped set kids on the right path to adulthood. Rather, rankings refer to national rankings, similar to the rankings of college teams. The similarity is hardly coincidental, for so much that drives the Youth Sports Industry is the hope of a coveted spot on a team at an elite college. To a surprising extent, pay-to-play sports can be viewed as farm programs for intercollegiate athletics, for the NCAA in particular. Keeping this in mind makes it less surprising that they have adopted many of the customs of intercollegiate athletics, including national rankings.

The MADLAX Lacrosse Club stresses on its website that it is the number one–ranked boys lacrosse club in Oregon. Included on the website is a link to the U.S. Club Lacrosse rankings of all club teams across the country for anyone who wants to verify MADLAX's claim. For some parents, if they are going to invest a large amount of money in a youth-sports club, better that it be the most elite club in the region, assuming that the most elite club will take one's child. Elite is one of the most common terms that pay-to-play clubs use, so much so that one wonders if the socioeconomic elite that provides the majority of participants in pay-to-play sports needs constant reassurance of its elite status.

With a few exceptions, any given club's tryouts are not advertised widely to the community in a way that attracts the best athletes to tryouts regardless of socioeconomic status. In most cases, the initial hurdle facing the youth athlete wanting to play competitive club sports is the ability of his or her family to pay. Once that criterion has been met, the club then turns its attention to evaluating the athlete in the child or, for older age groups, rating the candidate for competence in that specific sport.

As a basic rule, from among the pool of families who can pay, the more accomplished athletes are selected for the highest-level teams. Pay-to-play youth sports are mostly meritocratic within the select socioeconomic group that can afford the endeavor in the first place, but that corresponds to a small number of Americans overall. It is folly to think that the best American athletes are to be found only in the socioeconomically elite, but pay-to-play sports are largely limited to that class.

It is thus dubious for pay-to-play clubs to claim that they are contributing to, for example, the development of a specific sport in the United States when so much of the population is excluded from participation. This also raises grave ethical questions about colleges continuing to provide preferential admission to athletes at a time when athletics are increasingly a privilege of the wealthy. The pay-to-play club system is itself not entirely meritocratic even among those who can pay since within the socioeconomic elite there are those who have more to offer than the base fees. Some clubs extend an especially welcoming hand to families with the means and connections to help the club financially with donations and/or introductions to sponsors. In this area, too, the Youth Sports Industry has come to resemble how college athletics operates in that donations can be critically important. Do not underestimate the corruption factor in a youth-sports sector governed by market forces but almost entirely unregulated.

For the small group of Americans who have the resources and leisure time to focus on the national rankings of youth-sports clubs, these rankings loom large in the selection of a club, typically more so for the parents than for the players themselves. National rankings of club teams are one of the many aspects of youth sports that did not exist a generation ago. It would never have occurred to the players on a summer soccer-club team in the early 1980s that their team might be subjected to a national ranking. Considering that they never played any team who was not within a two-hour driving range, it is hard to imagine what the basis would have been for such rankings. But today national rankings are a big deal. They are marketing leverage to attract players. Just as there is a hierarchy of wine, with an industry to inform the consumer which wines have special cachet, there is a hierarchy in youth sports, with rankings to guide the consumer.

Rankings are also connected with the social-status aspect of pay-to-play sports—in other words, bragging rights. Rankings are also critically important for teams to gain access to elite tournaments and, once admitted, to be placed in the highest bracket (gold, silver, bronze, and so on) of competition. It ends up being a vicious circle. A team needs a good ranking to gain entrance into the desired bracket of a tournament, but the only way to achieve such a ranking is first to play and do well in numerous other tournaments, each of which tends to be costly and involve significant wear and tear on young bodies.

The MADLAX Lacrosse Club, on its website, also includes surprisingly honest verbiage about the environment in which it operates. It stresses that the result of its establishment through the merger of two clubs was "immediately becoming a major player in the Northwest lacrosse market." A generation ago, did people speak of the "youth soccer market" or the "youth volleyball market" or the "youth baseball market"? This sort of verbiage, as much as anything, indicates that what we now have in the United States is a Youth Sports Industry. It is also indicative of an environment whereby the market system has been extended to more and more areas of society. The market will determine which pay-to-play sports clubs are successful, but do we really believe that market success is what should determine which organizations provide opportunities for helping shape young athletes into responsible adults?

The dizzying number and frequency of mergers involving clubs, something we have witnessed in just the Portland metropolitan area, suggests the business climate in which they operate. These mergers almost always take place for business purposes rather than to, for example, provide more recreational-sports opportunities for youth in previously underserved neighborhoods. Successful clubs also license their prestigious name to clubs nationally and even internationally in a manner that parallels the franchising system used in many business sectors.

In the context of the Pacific Northwest, consider the description of the partnership between the Crossfire Premier Soccer Club (Redmond, Washington) and the Tualatin Hills United Soccer Club (Portland, Oregon) for the girls Elite Clubs National League component of THUSC: "Crossfire United ECNL is the elite program within the Tualatin Hills United Soccer Club. The Crossfire United brand is a collaboration between THUSC and Crossfire Premier." A generation ago, would it not have seemed strange for a youth-sports club to tout its "brand"?

What is coming together is not simply two clubs, one with a strong reputation at the regional and even national level. Rather, it is two clubs coming together in order to join another prestigious brand,

ECNL. ECNL, established in 2009, was in fact one of many newcomers in the past two decades to the world of youth soccer that now exists in parallel to United States Youth Soccer. ECNL's business model rests almost entirely on the promise that college coaches pay attention to ECNL, that by distinguishing themselves from less-elite teams, surely the coaches would recruit at ECNL competitions.

ECNL employs a system that evokes franchising, which not only promises consistency but also cachet. Across the United States, approximately 120 clubs with girls teams have gained entry into ECNL, which sponsors competitions between these club teams. ECNL recently adopted a two-tier system, grouping especially competitive teams in the first tier and less competitive teams in the second tier. There is now also a boys ECNL league with 140-plus clubs. Visibility to college soccer coaches through these competitions is arguably ECNL's most important selling point, but in the area of boys soccer in particular ECNL competes with several parallel leagues (e.g., MLS Next) for players and attention from college coaches. Even if we were to detail all the different pay-to-play leagues now in existence, it would likely be outdated quickly as the market is so fluid.

It is no coincidence that the E in ECNL stands for elite. The term is used so frequently in pay-to-play sports that all who seek to understand this sector must ponder why it is employed so often. What is it about this term that so many parents in particular and children, less so—but they may come to value it—find so seductive? In fact, the term elite is so pervasive in youth sports that one wonders if it is losing its value, eventually to be replaced by an acronym along the lines of EE, "elite of the elite." Those who have followed the evolution of youth sports would not be surprised if at some point a new supra-organization, EECNL, emerges and eclipses ECNL for allowing too many clubs to participate. After all, maintaining elite status requires exclusivity, and the very fact that the term elite has come to be used so frequently in the world of pay-to-play sports evidences how estranged this system is from providing sports opportunities to as many youth as possible.

In any case, the American elite wants to place its kids on elite club-sports teams. The goal, for some, is a spot on an elite team that regularly participates in elite tournaments where coaches from elite colleges will see them compete and hopefully recruit them. ECNL, for example, guards its brand and its logo, presumably hoping to maintain its elite status for as long as possible. According to the 2019–2020 ECNL Member Club Handbook:

Innovation, Excellence, & Player Development

The ECNL is the best female youth-soccer league in the United States and the most comprehensive elite female-development league in the world. This position is a reflection of the constant focus of ECNL on creating the most innovative, player-centered programming in female-soccer history. The ECNL is the aspirational focus for elite female athletes, and the ECNL brand is bold, innovative, and represents elite female athletic performance. The Style Guide is provided to ensure consistent and professional use of the ECNL logo throughout the country, in all ECNL Member Clubs, at all ECNL Competitions, and in all marketing and promotions related to ECNL. Use of any ECNL brand or logo must meet the requirements of this Style Guide.[17]

Once a club has gained entry into ECNL, it can then offer the franchised version of the ECNL brand. According to the 2021–22 ECNL Membership Agreement, a club must additionally promote ECNL as "the highest level of competition and player development in the United States." Article 4 of the terms of agreement includes the following warning: "If ECNL, in its reasonable discretion, believes that the Club at any point is not operating and promoting the ECNL Program as its highest level of competition and player development, such determination will constitute grounds for the immediate termination and/or nonrenewal of the Club's membership in ECNL's sole and absolute discretion." This is a nod to the fact that ECNL is hardly the only such youth-soccer league competing for membership and of its desire to keep the competition at bay.

Of course, each individual club must live up to its part of the bargain in other areas too. Although it is not quite analogous to serving French fries that taste more or less the same as those served at every other franchise location nationwide or even worldwide, what clubs, or franchises, must do in the case of ECNL is fulfill the requirements of having teams in several age groups participate in ECNL-sponsored competitions and along the way do things according to ECNL regulations. This represents, if one includes showcase tournaments and how far a team proceeds in the end-of-year ECNL championship tournaments, about 30 to 35 games per year per team. In more heavily populated regions of the country, a higher proportion of ECNL games may involve only local travel. But for clubs in regions with few if any other franchises, at least half of the games require plane travel to a location where several ECNL teams are brought together for a "weekend" of games. And although games tend to take place on Saturdays and Sundays, travel on Fridays and Mondays can be part of the equation, meaning missed school.

One of the many curious aspects of pay-to-play sports is the notion that missed school days are acceptable collateral damage for what is more important, namely tournaments and other competitions. This is one aspect of the Youth Sports Industry that is definitely new compared to a generation ago. It is an aspect that shocks and amazes many older parents, but younger parents seem to have accepted it as the norm. Unsurprisingly, most child participants do not complain about the missed school days.

ECNL provides on its website a form that parents can submit to schools explaining absences. The form emphasizes the tremendous significance of these competitions, even while stressing the lengths ECNL takes to minimize the number of school days missed. Then why schedule games early on Saturdays or late on Sundays? ECNL explains, in regretful language, that participants occasionally must miss school but only for a worthy reason. According to the 2021–22 form letter:

> ECNL works diligently to limit the number of school days missed due to participation in ECNL National Events. However, it is impossible to eliminate all school absences. Each ECNL National Event occurs over a weekend (either Friday–Sunday or Saturday–Monday), but due to the need to travel across the country for these events, student-athletes may have to miss an additional day of school for each event. Occasionally, travel for regional games (regular-season games) may require the student-athletes to miss part of a Friday school day. We ask for your understanding in this matter and your support of these student-athletes as they attempt to continue their careers in college and beyond.[18]

Parents are not necessarily incorrect in calculating that the visibility to college coaches provided by these competitions may increase the likelihood of a spot on a team at an elite college more than regular attendance at school, but only if their child is highly proficient at a sport.

Colleges and universities have not taken issue with the leagues that require youth to miss school. After all, it is the presence of coaches under their employment who justify these tournaments for which kids are sacrificing school attendance. Institutions of higher education could ban their coaches from recruiting at any sort of youth competition that results in players missing school in order to attend. And this distinctly American mixing of academics and athletics at the college level is migrating to younger and younger age groups, in some cases in a form of athletics more intense and demanding than at the college level itself. Ask typical college athletes to compare how many games they play to how many they played while involved in pay-to-play before college and most all will say that the number of college games represents only a fraction of games compared to what their pay-to-play youth sport required. This contrast further calls into question the overwhelming practice and game schedules of many pay-to-play youth-sports clubs.

Winning and Getting Your Spot on a College Team

A key selling point of almost all clubs, as well as national leagues such as ECNL, is their track record in placing athletes on college teams. This often overlaps with national rankings, but whether or not a club is able to tout a national ranking it will highlight its success in placing players on college teams. Some observers mistakenly connect the dream chasing involved in the Youth Sports Industry only to the professional sports leagues. Although the dream of playing professionally is part of the story, most families involved in the Youth Sports Industry are more driven by the preferential admission that colleges grant to athletes.

The Portland Volleyball Club in Oregon, not a particularly renowned club, nonetheless includes a hall of fame on its website composed of every alumnus who ever went on to play in college. This club's featuring of alumni who went on is restrained compared to those of more-famous clubs. It simply lists the names of the alumni with no photos or additional razzmatazz. Clubs almost never feature alumni who did not play the sport in college yet went on to do great things with their lives. These clubs claim to foster the development of values and lessons important to life overall, so why not highlight examples of how their alumni have put those values to work in sectors outside athletics?

Playing in college, earning a spot on a college team, all the better if at an elite college, is the holy grail sought after from pay-to-play sports, especially by parents, and also, as they get older, by the youth participants. So, it is not surprising from a basic marketing perspective that almost all clubs highlight in one way or another their college success stories. Clubs must provide evidence that they send players on to compete at the college level. Parents want evidence of this, evidence of return on investment. More-famous clubs may be able to feature alumni who have gone on to play professionally, but most of the focus is on the coveted spot on a college team.

If the club has had a player who went on to play for the national team, that is a marketing dream come true, and that player will likely be featured most prominently. That is the sort of hook to get parents salivating about the potential return on investment. Clubs have also come to employ Twitter, Instagram, Facebook, and other social media to announce the signings of their players to college teams as well as other exploits by club players, teams, and alumni that hype the club. Increasingly, news of a club team's championship at a tournament, whatever the age group, is immediately trumpeted through social-media posts.

The return-on-investment angle is highlighted prominently. For example, the Orlando Tampa Volleyball Club specifically stresses that its "goal is to provide the highest return for your investment." Considering the costs associated with playing club sports, it is difficult to fault parents for viewing it as an investment from which a return should be expected.

But, again, it seems like a strange term to use in reference to participation in youth sports, further evidence of how marketing has penetrated pay-to-play. Parents seeking a return on investment may want to familiarize themselves with the statistics about how few youth athletes ever play in college, if that is the return on investment they have in mind. In his book "Changing the Game," John O'Sullivan provides some sobering statistics about the gap between the percentage of parents who believe their children are good enough to play in college (30 to 50 percent) and how many high-school athletes actually go on to play in college (3 to 5 percent).

If parents approached the question of return on investment analytically, really asking themselves what were the chances their 6-year-old would end up playing in college, they would very possibly conclude that most clubs are selling something akin to snake oil. But the simple fact that colleges do offer preferential admissions as well as scholarships to athletes is fundamental to the Youth Sports Industry.

If parents approach participation on a team from a different perspective, then it is still possible to be satisfied with return on investment from the growth as an individual that their child experiences through participation in sports. But shouldn't there be far more affordable youth-sports opportunities available to all? Learning life lessons as a return for a minimal financial investment would be a better outcome for most everyone involved.

Crossfire Premier uses curious verbiage to stress that evaluations of Crossfire teams and players must go beyond the wins and losses in soccer. According to its vision statement on its website: "Crossfire Premier aims to field boys and girls teams that stand out even among the most successful in America, not solely due to results but also made remarkable by the playing product our players put on display." What is a "playing product"? A product such as detergent is supposed to clean clothes. But what is "playing product" in the world of pay-to-play sports, in this case soccer?

Presumably it is the style of soccer that Crossfire Premier teams are taught to play. Does that mean the Crossfire player not only knows when to pass but also when to dribble, when to hustle to do a quick throw-in to catch the opposing team off guard and when to take the throw-in more deliberately in order to allow teammates to regain their formation? Youth sports is developing a whole new marketing nomenclature.

Increasingly the focus on websites is achievement of younger and younger athletes, as in highlighting U-14-level players invited to national training camps. One Oregon baseball club, Moundtime, stresses the many championships its teams have won. Almost all pay-to-pay clubs engage in rhetoric about the importance of developing players over winning, but the winning part of the equation is crucial to business success. Almost all clubs that want to attract players must demonstrate short-term success in competition, winning today, not developing players who will play the game properly down the road and win because they mastered the basics.

Any parent who has been through pay-to-play sports with even one child almost surely has a story of the early developer, an account of the kid whose growth spurt preceded that of peers and who was so obviously used by the club to try to win at, say, the U-11 level only to be discarded in later years when the size advantage was no longer in play. What makes some of these cases especially egregious is the failure of the club to insist that the early developer learn basic skills along the way rather than rely on size advantage for the short-term benefit of the club more than the long-term benefit of the player.

Such cases are so frequent that they are almost instantaneously recognizable in any youth sport. Who cares about victories at this age? Well, clubs care because winning attracts players, and winning leads to higher national rankings, which also attracts more players. Parents of early developers should be doubly wary of this scenario and especially adamant that their kids be taught basic skills rather than be relied on for short-lived advantages that come with early development. So which is it going to be, pay-to-play clubs, development or winning?

When our daughters played for one of the local pay-to-play soccer clubs in Portland, players received generally equal playing time for most of the year except when the State Cup came around. Even for the youngest ages, this club made clear that the goal was to win the State Cup, end of discussion. The State Cup consists of club teams competing at their respective age groups to win the highest level of the state championship or cup, which then allows teams at older ages to advance to regionals and from there perhaps to nationals. Coaches sent a long message, recycled each year as the State Cup approached, alerting families that playing time would not be equal in State Cup games and that there was no guarantee of some kids playing at all during certain games. Also, clubs, should a team advance to regionals, can replace players who helped them win the State Cup with better players within the club. This is within the rules, but it hardly fosters a sense of team spirit and seems incredibly inappropriate at the youth level.

The goal of winning the State Cup is clearly a financial decision more than a child-development issue. Clubs typically advertise the number of State Cups won at different ages prominently on their web-sites, and families quickly come to understand that this is an import-ant measure of a club under the present system. This is true although the value of the State Cup has diminished in recent years. Up until the early twenty-first century, specifically until the establishment of U.S. Club Soccer in 2001, almost no clubs traveled out of state for games. Winning the State Cup was the one route to gaining entry to a tour-nament, namely Regionals (and if one won Regionals one advanced to Nationals), that featured clubs from numerous states. The U.S. Club Soccer model was unregulated and market based, and this subse-quently led to the explosion of the for-profit club soccer sector. There are so many different leagues and tournaments these days that provide for inter-state competition that some clubs no longer bother with the State Cup competition, although winning it still carries some cachet.

We have never come across a successful (defined as attracting plen-tiful players) pay-to-play club that without exception puts development first, often leaving parents to try to find the club with the "least worst" practices. The entire system makes it next to impossible to consistently choose development over winning. And the temptations are endless.

Many pay-to-play sports-club websites include photos of young athletes, sometimes surprisingly young, hoisting the championship trophy. Winning sells. But what really sells is winning combined with placing kids on college teams. Successful pay-to-play clubs tend to partner with one of the college-athlete placement services in order to help guide parents and players through the process of landing a spot on a college team. Sometimes it is a requirement for families on club teams to sign up with one of the college-sports recruiting companies (it makes one wonder if the clubs receive kickbacks). But some of the larger clubs have been able to develop their own college-placement arm, with an in-house "college-program administrator" offered as a free perk to paying members of the club. The description of the ser-vices offered is similar to the college-placement services offered by elite private schools, which is not surprising since such clubs generally serve families of similar socioeconomic status.

Coach-administrators in the world of pay-to-play club soccer do not operate in silos. They pay attention to what is working, in a business sense, for other clubs. The mission statement of the organization United Soccer Coaches defines it as "the trusted and unifying voice, advocate, and partner for coaches of all levels of the game." United Soccer Coaches undeniably has a strong educational focus—to develop better soccer coaches. One regular attendee of the the organization's annual conference, which typically takes place in January, informed us that after the day's official coach-training sessions are over, the talk among many of the participants, especially those who own and/or administer pay-to-play clubs, turns to sharing intelligence on the business side of running a club and how to maximize profit.

The focus on playing in college and gaining preferential admission is substantially an American phenomenon. Make no mistake that elite professional clubs in other countries have youth academies devoted to developing players for their clubs as well as armies of scouts to scour the world for prospects. But professional academies outside the United States typically pay all of the expenses, including travel expenses, for their youth athletes and their coaches alike. Compared to their American pay-to-play counterparts, the potential for conflicts of interest involving parents, donors, and sponsors is reduced dramatically. The singular focus is identifying and grooming the extraordinarily rare kids who will one day play in the first professional division. In contrast, the American obsession with placing youth on college teams is not replicated in its scope and intensity anywhere else in the world.

When Americans try to explain the significance and prestige of having a child on a college-athletics team to people outside the United States, they are often met with bafflement. The reason is that for people most everywhere else in the world playing sports in college imparts next to no status. Foreigners unfamiliar with the American system of college sports will likely interpret participation on an American college-sports team to be hardly any different from, say, taking part in a hiking club that one finds at colleges worldwide. For most of the rest of the world, sports are divided into professional and recreational, without the college sector that looms so large in the United States. Preferential admission to college on the basis of athletics is unthinkable in much of the rest of the world, where admission is typically exam based.

However, American college coaches have more and more come to recruit internationally, and in fact winning or losing at the college level in many sports increasingly depends on supplementing American talent with overseas players. This seems an especially strange practice when it comes to public American universities, but somehow the fact that universities supported by taxpayer money are scouring the planet for, say, volleyball players who might win them a national championship rarely becomes an issue. In 2021, the Oregon State University men's soccer team played the University of Portland's team. Every single starter for Oregon State came from outside of North America. Do not get us wrong, the fact that for decades American universities have attracted numerous foreign students has been beneficial on so many fronts. But it does seem more than a little strange that the men's soccer team of a state university would field a starting lineup that did not include even a single American player.

The global elite is wising up to the American system. At the Harvard College Boys Soccer ID camp in 2021, families came from numerous foreign countries including Japan, Brazil, and Turkey. ID camps are what they sound like—a means for coaches to identify promising players. ID camps are also major moneymakers for college coaches. The hope of participating families was that their teenage son would attract the attention of the Harvard coaches and earn a designated spot on the team, which typically results in preferential admission as long as the academics fit within a far broader range than one might expect for the elite college.

The Three Tiers of Pay-to-Play

In the American Youth Sports Industry, who are the faces, besides the players, who make up a typical pay-to-play sports club? And what do they earn? Broadly speaking, there are three tiers of pay-to-play youth-sports clubs. Although the following is based on soccer clubs, it holds true for many other pay-to-play sports. Tier 1 consists of clubs that year after year can field nationally competitive teams at every age group, or at least most age groups. Unsurprisingly, these clubs represent a small percentage of the overall number of clubs and tend to be concentrated in areas with large populations, such as metropolitan areas and their suburbs.

In girls soccer, tier 1 clubs would not necessarily include all the clubs that are participating in ECNL. Rather, it would include those that consistently, at multiple age groups, place teams in the upper-tier championship tournament at the end of the ECNL season, the result of having done well during the regular league games. In every way imaginable, from infrastructure to salaries, the elite clubs are in a different class from almost all other clubs. Their marketing niche consists of those families looking for the most "elite" experience possible.

Families are known to drive for hours to get kids to practices at these clubs, even to fly them to practices. Participants on such elite teams, if they participate on their high-school teams, are likely the stars, though many club coaches recommend that their players not "waste their time" playing on the high-school team, and certain clubs (some of which call themselves academies) actually forbid participation on high-school teams. On some especially elite teams, every player earns a spot on a college roster, or could earn a spot on a team at some college, putting aside whether it is a good match for the player.

The key for a club to earn and maintain its status as a tier 1 club is the performance, year after year, of its highest-level teams in each age group. Almost all tier 1 clubs have multiple teams at each age group, so the number of players registered can be significant. This requires a correspondingly large staff. Kids mature at different ages, and having teams of different levels does provide for movement, both upward and downward in terms of the level of the team that any given youth makes at the time of the annual tryouts. But the prestige of the club rests on results by its top-level teams in the different age groups in major competitions, not in the number of youth participating in that club's activities or, for that matter, on the performance of the B-, C-, and D-level teams. Some tier 1 clubs capitalize on the prestige earned by the club's top teams to attract large pools of players overall, so tier 1 clubs can be elite but also deep in terms of numbers, an attractive business model. For example, North Carolina FC (NCFC) has more than 10,000 registered players, with revenues of more than $13 million according to its 990 filing (the public tax return that is required of all non-profits) from 2020.

The second tier of clubs includes some young athletes who will go on to play college sports. Reasons that some of the better players in tier 2 clubs are not on tier 1 clubs range from geography (too long a commute) to the fact that some teenagers are not willing to make one sport their singular activity, a level of commitment that in terms of hours involved can be little different from a full-time job. Second-tier teams also include many players who would not make the top team at the tier 1 clubs. Although some tier 2 teams might have one or two quite good players, along with a supporting cast of above-average athletes, they would likely get clobbered by one of the truly elite club teams.

Successful tier 2 clubs cast a wide net in terms of attracting players. They can find plentiful opportunities, including endless tournaments, that offer a competitive pay-to-play sports experience. Some of the participants on tier 2 teams might be star players on their high-school teams whereas others would likely secure a spot on the varsity team of a large public school by, say, their junior year.

The third tier of clubs basically offers, in terms of the "quality of play" (another phrase that was far less bandied about in the pre-professionalized age of youth sports), something closer to a recreational-sports experience. But the fees are typically far beyond that of the local little leagues, in no small part because the sport takes place year-round. The athletes are expected to buy uniform kits. The coaching staff tends to be paid, but there are no illusions about competing in elite tournaments. Nonetheless, there are numerous league games, tournaments, and other opportunities to play the sport.

Participating in tier 3 clubs helps some of the players make their high-school squads, depending on how competitive the high-school team is. One of the many ways that pay-to-play sports have changed the overall landscape for youth sports in the United States is that it can be surprisingly difficult, even impossible, in most sports for a kid to secure a spot even on a public high-school team unless he or she has been playing pay-to-play club sports from a young age. This is especially true at larger high schools. Having played on a tier 3 club, even from a young age, may not be sufficient to make the cut at some high schools, but it can increase the likelihood of success. In order to try keeping the high-school-sports playing field somewhat level, the Ohio High School Athletic Association now limits to five the number of players on the high-school team who can be on the same club team. Otherwise, certain high-school teams could enjoy an incredibly high concentration of players from the same club team, making the high-school season somewhat of an extension of the club season, at least for a few elite high schools.

Even parents who have no illusions about their children earning spots on college teams but who remember how taking part in high-school sports was meaningful for themselves and helped direct them away from destructive activities feel that they must "invest" in pay-to-play sports so that their kids will be able to make the cut at the high-school level. This development is a decidedly distasteful side effect of the growth of pay-to-play for those who believe sports should serve as a means to compress, rather than enlarge, the societal differences brought on by the wealth gap. Almost no one from tier 3 will go on to play in college, although there are always exceptions, but at least they may get to participate in high-school sports.

For all three of the tiers of soccer clubs, player fees make up a significant portion of the revenue, and personnel salaries make up a significant portion of the expenses. Player fees can range from $1,000 to $4,000 annually depending on numerous factors, including location. Remember, however, that player fees are simply the base cost of pay-to-play sports; they do not cover travel, which is fundamental to participating at the tier 1 level and often even at the tier 2 level. Tier 2 and tier 3 clubs typically cannot charge as much for player fees as their elite counterparts, but if they are skillful at marketing then they can attract large numbers of players. The business model is to attract as many players as possible, the equivalent of selling simple sliced white bread to large numbers of consumers rather than selling multigrain bread at a premium to a smaller number of consumers. But it is also true that having nationally successful teams can also help some clubs attract a deep pool of players, although only a quarter or so of the players in such a club might be competing at the elite level.

Sponsorships, Fund-Raising, and Conflicts of Interest

The higher the prestige of the club, the more likely that it can access and generate additional sources of revenue from sponsors, donors, and events such as tournaments. In the same way that the practice of national rankings has migrated down from college sports to youth-club sports, the practice of various businesses sponsoring college pro-grams has extended down to youth sports. Elite youth-sports clubs can line up significant sponsorships, with individual sponsorships in some cases in the tens of thousands or even hundreds of thousands of dollars.

Sponsorship of youth sports has itself become an industry. For example, companies in the athletic-wear sector can justify sponsor-ships of clubs and tournaments in order to gain early converts (e.g., kids in Nike uniforms and footwear), who will go on to provide lifelong revenue streams ("I have been wearing Adidas since I was a kid."). At times, sponsorship takes curious forms from the perspective of players' families. For example, families are required to purchase, annually or every other year, uniform kits manufactured by the club sponsor, which for soccer are in the $350 range (including matching sweatshirt and sweatpants). In early 2022, F.C. Portland in Oregon sent out an email to families explaining that the club had transitioned to a new local soccer store for providing the uniform kits. Without the slightest mention of cost, the email stressed, "For the 2022–2023 season we will have a brand-new Nike kit and training-gear options for our players."

Why it is necessary for youth teams to be outfitted hardly any differently from their professional counterparts leads in part to the bottom line of various sportswear companies. It also relates to the prestige and status factors now connected to youth sports, with uniforms serving as advertisements for who plays for which club, a contemporary status symbol.

Many parents have wondered if the athletic companies make more revenue, perhaps even far more revenue, from the uniform kits that they offer through their sponsorships of youth-sports clubs. When our daughters were with one club that was sponsored by Nike, we regularly received emails from the administrative head of the club expressing his shock and disappointment at having seen kids wearing shoes other than Nikes in recent games and practices (strictly speaking, the club did not require its players to wear Nike footwear, but the administrative head did his best to communicate a "moral imperative" in this area). Our oldest daughter remembers to this day how extraordinarily angry her club coaches would get if players did not come to practice wearing "official club gear," which included the logo of a major sportswear company. As she got older she began to tell them that she would wear such gear without fail only if it were provided to her for free because it had nothing to do with her desire to develop as a soccer player.

From the perspective of the participating families, are the sponsors earning far more than they are giving in sponsorships, even though the amount can vary from four digits to six digits and maybe even seven with particularly famous clubs? Or is the relationship more along the lines of "forced consumerism." In any case, sponsorship of clubs by companies typically involves significant extraction of resources from families in the form of required purchases, whatever the sponsorship means to the club in other areas.

For coaches, sponsorship by an athletic-wear company often means that they receive voluminous "swag," ranging from all-weather gear—multiple coats to suit the season since pay-to-play sports are year-round—to sometimes footwear and balls and other equipment. This gear can easily be worth $1,000. Club administrators may enjoy even greater benefits. This practice is a valuable marketing tool for the sponsor rather than a simple donation, necessary and useful as balls and other equipment are. The coaches, some of whom might be admired former professionals, are figures of authority, and often kids want to emulate them. This makes coaches into billboards for sports-wear companies.

Pay-to-play sports clubs often employ a CEO or someone in another position whose job description includes signing up significant sponsors. Sponsors of youth-sports clubs tend to be in the sporting industry but can include almost any type of company, especially if it is a company with a mass-consumption product. It is not unusual for a sponsorship deal to include the sponsor having its name and logo on the uniforms as well as perhaps the backpacks or other types of bags and other equipment of all of the players for that club. One need spend only a few hours at a tournament in the Portland area to see jerseys with logos of U.S. Bank, Buffalo Wild Wings, or Directors Mortgage. A tournament in Orlando, Florida, included team sponsorships by Cheez-It and InStat.

Parents with kids in pay-to-play clubs are so accustomed to seeing even U-11 kids running around in uniforms advertising sponsors that they have become inured to whether 10-year-old boys and girls should be serving as human billboards. Or perhaps the inclusion of sponsor logos on uniforms makes it seem all the more professional.

Pay-to-play sports are by definition geared toward the socio-economic elite, and the more elite clubs tend to attract a particu-larly disproportionate number of members of the elite of the elite. Unsurprisingly, as nonprofits, these clubs target these families for tax-deductible donations. As with so much about American society, the advantages of association with the rich are often compounded. Parents who hold high-level jobs in highly successful private corporations often can have their personal donations to nonprofit organizations matched up to a set amount by the employer. Only a tiny percentage

of American corporations are willing to match their employees' donations, but it is a common practice among those privileged to work for
especially successful companies such as Adidas and Intel.

Elite clubs often have regular and sophisticated fund-raising operations targeting private donors. It does not take much to understand
the sort of conflicts of interest that such practices can produce, and not
all clubs have firewalls in place to neutralize these conflicts of interest.
For instance, imagine that a player's family is a generous donor to the
club, but as the player gets older his or her playing ability no longer justifies inclusion on the top-level team for the age group. But if
the player is dropped from that team, what becomes of that family's
annual donation?

There are worse scenarios. Imagine if key donor parents threaten
to leave the club if their child does not start every game and get more
playing time than any other player. Sports, one area where merit tends
to display itself on the field of competition, can be corrupted from
the amount of money now invested at the youth level and the stakes
involved in colleges privileging athletes for admissions and in an especially small number of cases, scholarships.

The Varsity Blues scandal of 2019, in which parents offered bribes
to college coaches and administrators to get their supposedly athletic
children—whose backgrounds in sports were fabricated—admitted to
elite institutions such as the University of Southern California (USC) is
one such shameful by-product of the present system of college admissions on which so much of the Youth Sports Industry depends. Illegal
though it was, the threads of the Varsity Blues scam nonetheless speak
to the fact that athletic prowess as well as donations, sometimes in
combination, unquestionably grease the admissions process at elite
schools.

Another conflict of interest is when parents with a player in a club
are influential in arranging for a sponsor. Anger that family, and the
club jeopardizes a lucrative sponsorship. Even cases when parents
are asked to contribute to what would seem the worthiest of causes,
namely providing a scholarship so a deserving player from a family

that is not part of the socioeconomic elite can play, can cause problems. Imagine that the family of player A is underwriting the participation of player B, a player with true promise. By the time the tryouts approach, it is clear that player A no longer merits inclusion on the top team. But the club is eager to keep player B. Financially the only way to keep player B may be to retain player A on the top team even if player A is undeserving in terms of playing ability.

Then there are the various methods parents use to "cultivate" their relationship with the coach and club administrators, which can include expensive gifts such as front-row seats to the local NBA team's games or invitations to golf at a ritzy course. Why doesn't every pay-to-play club across the land institute and enforce strict policies forbidding parents from gifting anything to employees of the club? Pay-to-play clubs, with their nonprofit status, typically have boards, which in theory, and sometimes in practice, provide a collective voice of reason to the operations of the club. But these boards frequently consist of parents of players in the club who often have agendas centered on their own children. Thus boards, seemingly the solution to the problem, themselves can be the source of conflicts of interest. This is in fact one of the underlying reasons driving the move toward private ownership of clubs.

One of the most flagrant conflicts of interest we saw firsthand involved a local college coach who also coached the local club team, which he clearly sought to use as a farm team for his college program. This particular coach declined to share with one of the gifted female soccer players under his tutelage the fact that numerous other college programs were interested in her, not until she had committed to his program. He also declined to help any player investigate the possibility of playing at any program other than his own. This was a major problem for players in the club because it is common for college coaches, as the first step in the recruiting process that includes NCAA rules regulating when they can reach out directly to players, to contact coaches at the club when they have become interested in a player. This coach flat out declined to help players from this club realize their dreams to play at college programs other than his own. This coach also steered his college players away from demanding majors such as nursing at his institution that might get in the way of soccer. He would often give speeches to the youth players about how it was imperative that they devote themselves only to soccer year-round, an equation that also financially benefited him, rather than play multiple sports, even as he had no intention of covering the costs of the resulting overuse injuries. Curiously, this hypocritical coach had himself played multiple sports as a kid.

Justice eventually caught up with the coach. After having driven a famous college program with two national championships to its credit into the ground, he was fired from his college coaching position. Before long he was also fired from his youth-club coaching position for mistreating players. The warning signs of his willingness to ignore boundaries had been there for years, and yet the club proved incapable of putting proper firewalls in place.

Following the Money

The economics of youth sports also includes tournaments, the subject of Chapter Three, which tend to be phenomenal moneymakers. But as lucrative as tournaments can be, for most clubs they do not match the importance of player fees. Tier 1 clubs can of course charge higher player fees. That main source of revenue combined with donations, sponsorships, and successful tournaments, can provide for salaries that allow both administrators and coaches to make youth sports their full-time jobs. It is not unusual for the CEO of an elite club as well as other key positions such as director of coaching, to make more than six figures annually. At some clubs, to get to above $100,000 annually, a director of coaching may have also to serve as head coach of a team, thus combining that salary with the director of coaching salary. Head coaches may get paid as much as $30,000 per team, and some coaches are able to juggle as many as three teams. An assistant coach will make approximately half that of the head coach.

Add into the equation a head coach who tops off that salary by offering supplemental training camps for serious young athletes (e.g.,

Agility and Fitness), organizing summer camps, which can be especially lucrative and also predate the pay-to-play model, although the astonishing fees that prestigious camps now charge represent something new, and by tutoring players for as much as $100 per hour (hourly sports tutorial fees can run as high as $200 per hour), and that coach can easily make more than $100,000 annually. Additionally, fees received for tutoring players are frequently received in cash, but it makes one wonder how much of if any of that income is reported to the IRS.

Such earnings potential in youth sports represents quite a difference from a generation ago when almost all youth-sports coaches were volunteers. Obviously there is nothing inherently wrong with youth coaches getting paid a decent salary, and more and more clubs are moving toward coaches as employees rather than as independent contractors. In fact, a system that ensured that youth-sports coaches could make a decent living would attract good coaches for the long term. According to market-system principles, it makes total sense that coaches are capitalizing on the demand by the elite for pay-to-play sports. But the fact that youth sports are increasingly left to the market is precisely the problem.

The market-based Youth Sports Industry serves only a small percentage of overall youth, even as its success ("Look at all those kids using all those playing fields!") provides a mirage suggesting that all is healthy with youth sports in the United States when it is not. Behind the mirage of so many kids playing on so many fields is the fact that fields, at least decent ones, are only sparsely available for recreational sports. Another problem is that many families who make great sacrifices so their children can participate in a pay-to-play sport have no idea just how much various representatives of the club are making off the endeavor even as they ask the families for ever more volunteer time and ever more monetary contributions to finance yet another travel tournament.

The coach of one of our daughter's club teams once simply announced that the team would be traveling to Italy. This was a bald move by a coach presumably looking for a free trip to Europe. After initial attempts at fund-raising produced results that were ludicrous in terms of the amount of money raised in comparison to parental hours expended, several families rebelled and quashed the coach's plans, a rare reining in of the coach's expectations that the parents would finance everything he expected of them. Let this serve as a caveat to parents. If a club proposes some expensive trip that is drawing some resistance from parents and then the topic of fund-raising is introduced to alleviate anxiety about the cost, do not be fooled. Unless the club plans on going out and finding a major sponsor for the trip, the fund-raising will prove to be a flop. But by the time it becomes evident that fund-raising is not going to defray the cost of the trip in any meaningful way, planning for the trip may be so far along that the parents may be on the hook for its cost all the same.

If more parents who are frequently implored to volunteer on behalf of clubs had a better sense of what club administrators and coaches earn, they might be a little less willing to volunteer. One of the most ironic instances of clubs pleading parents to volunteer is to help make tournaments run smoothly. On the other hand, in the minds of many parents, volunteering can be a means to "get in good with the club and/or coach," thereby perhaps giving one's child an edge.

One of the clubs in the Portland metropolitan area that has proven in our minds to be the most ethically managed across the board compensates the field marshals necessary to ensure that tournaments run smoothly. Considering that one of the most important duties of the field marshal is to monitor parental behavior and intervene with those acting inappropriately—potentially volatile work—this job deserves compensation. Of course, most of the field marshals end up being parents, but at least this practice transcends systems designed for clubs to maximize tournament profits on the back of volunteer labor. Parents should insist that all labor in support of pay-to-play tournaments be compensated.

There is another way of looking at the phenomenon of paid coaches. There is no doubt that the fact coaches can now make a living wage keeps some great coaches on the sidelines longer than might otherwise have been the case. We encountered a few truly great coaches along the way in pay-to-play soccer, even as mediocrity was more the norm. But one could argue that the pay has now reached a level that it keeps many individuals in coaching who simply could not earn a commensurate standard of living otherwise—parasites who have latched on to the upper 20 percent or so of Americans who can afford pay-to-play sports.

It is obvious to anyone who has been involved with pay-to-play soccer that there are coaches who apparently are doing it largely for the money. They go through the motions of coaching, showing little passion, failing to take actions against problematic players, and generally not teaching their players much of anything about the game of soccer or life. Many are first and foremost looking for the next club to join that will pay them even more money. Coaching youth sports requires a deep, multidimensional skill set, far more so than most people realize. Knowing the game is not enough. Communication skills are essential. An understanding of child development is imperative. The list is long. Depending on the definition of what constitutes "a great coach," it's doubtful that the professionalization of pay-to-play youth sports has increased the percentage of great coaches.

To be sure, these days coaching at a pay-to-play club can be quite demanding, often involving extensive travel, not to mention the pressure to win. If one gets almost any decent pay-to-play youth-sports coach talking about the culture of pay-to-play sports, he or she will quickly list a litany of improvements they would like to make. Almost without exception, however, the number-one complaint tends to be having to deal with overbearing parents.

Toward the end of the first year that our oldest daughter played pay-to-play soccer, we heard the team manager, an endlessly upbeat woman, make a comment that suggested there had been a parental complaint about something. We asked her if the parents complained much, and she looked at us as though we must be the most naive people on the face of the earth. She had dealt with endless parental complaints throughout the year regarding a team of 10-year old girls. The complaints culminated in quite a to-do right at the end of the season in reference to the one and only travel tournament for that age group. There was a girl whose family's religious beliefs did not permit her to play in the Saturday games. Multiple parents made it abundantly clear where they stood about the possibility that the coaches might provide a little extra playing time in Sunday's games to that player. The coaches never gave the slightest indication that they might provide the girl with extra playing time in Sunday's games, but the parents were thinking ahead about this possibility and wanted to preempt it. There is a synergy involving multiple actors that produces the culture, for good and for bad, of pay-to-play youth sports.

Tier 1 clubs are typically in a better position to invest significantly in nurturing their coaching staff, which over time should result in a staff with a better knowledge of how to teach the sport but by no means guarantees a higher-quality staff in the area of teaching life lessons. Such clubs typically employ a full-time director of coaching whose job responsibilities include developing a curriculum for each age group and also ensuring that the coaches are trained to implement the curriculum. Coaches typically learn from other coaches.

Additionally, tier 1 clubs are typically in a position to pay the costs, either entirely or at least partially, of their coaching staff earning the various levels of coaching licenses offered by the national organization in the sport (many but not all sports have licensing systems for coaches). These licenses are meaningful. They do in some sense indicate whether a coach knows the sport, but less well whether or not they can teach it. But rarely do they measure if a coach is prepared to tend to the emotions of 9-year olds and other developmental issues. If one includes travel and lodging expenses in addition to registration fees, the cost of proceeding all the way through to the highest-level license in soccer can easily top $20,000. Coaches with higher-level licenses are typically in a position to receive higher salaries and also compete for the most desirable coaching positions.

Although it is still rare, some clubs have established a level of economic security and continuity that allow them to offer benefits such as health insurance to their entire staff, including coaches. Most of the clubs that can do this are in tier 1. This is further evidence of how much pay-to-pay-clubs have come to resemble successful businesses, in these cases ones that endeavor to treat their employees well. It's doubtful if even one of the volunteer coaches who a generation ago got themselves to the field to coach after a demanding day of work ever imagined that within another generation it would be possible to make a six-figure salary with benefits from coaching youth sports. Although travel to tournaments is demanding time-wise, the regular weekly schedule is comparatively cushy. It includes two 90-minute or 120-minute practices and two games that take place locally on the weekend for a total of about eight hours of work.

How are coaches at tier 1 clubs evaluated? Almost all pay-to-play clubs offer up a surfeit of flowery rhetoric about nurturing citizenship, development over winning, and sportsmanship, which comes across as impressive to parents at first but increasingly nonsensical as they become aware of the realities of pay-to-play clubs. The reality frequently conflicts with these lofty goals. When all is said and done, coaches at tier 1 clubs are judged by their win/loss record. Tier 1 clubs must win to maintain their tier 1 status. It is as simple as that.

Whether or not a coach who has been successful in winning will also be judged on the basis of how he or she went about winning (was it a positive experience for the players?) depends on the club. Many well-run clubs quickly rid themselves of negative, abusive coaches, but at the same time it is through winning that a club earns tier 1 status. Long before money was a factor in youth sports, in the name of winning at all costs, there was poor behavior by coaches, parents, and occasionally players, and there was also cheating.

None of those and other ills is new to pay-to-play sports. What is new is the amount of money that is now related to winning, to earning and keeping tier 1 status. There is financial profit to be gained by winning in youth sports, something that was almost entirely absent a generation ago, and this adds an additional pressure on coaches. At this point in time, some youth-sports coaches face economic pressures to win that are no different than their college and professional counterparts in the sense that they may lose their positions and their livelihoods otherwise. The focus on winning extends down to the youngest age groups. Our oldest daughter, who is now a coach, reminds us that even at the youngest age groups players are forced to play in formations and listen to complex half-time talks although they are not developmentally ready to gain anything from these rituals.

The extraordinary focus on winning does not always encourage behavior by coaches that is in the best interest of young players. A coach at the U-12 level may practice his players day after day without rest to a level of performance rare for that age. The team may go on to win various championships (tournaments, State Cup, Regionals, and perhaps even Nationals) that year, earning a place on the club's website for a photo featuring the hoisting of the trophy. But later, overuse injuries may fell members of the team one by one, injuries for which the coach who over-practiced them at the U-12 level bears some responsibility but who will likely never be held accountable.

While such a coach is busy over-practicing a different group of prepubescent youth, parents and players perhaps fail to connect the dots between the overuse that began at a young age and the devastating injury that eventually takes place. That coach has basically behaved in a neglectful manner toward his players, setting them up for injuries that can take a year to rehabilitate at extraordinary expense or which may even end their playing careers at a young age. Of course, there are certain parents who not only support but also indeed demand this approach to coaching and perhaps even find what many professionals consider to be over practicing still to be insufficient.

At tier 2 clubs, the economic situation is quite different. There may be only one employee making more than six figures. Although this individual is typically referred to as the "director" of the club, that position is not necessarily different from the owner of a for-profit business. At the end of the fiscal year, any profit earned by a regular business belongs to the owner(s). In the case of 501(c)(3) nonprofit organizations, when revenues exceed expenses in any given fiscal year, the difference (in essence, profit, although that term is typically avoided) belongs to the club. But this simply means that the director or directors running the club, in order to disburse that profit to themselves, must take the extra step of paying themselves, as salary, part or all of the portion of revenue that exceeded expenses.

In practice, 501(c)(3) organizations can provide quite a healthy livelihood to those who manage them. Consider, for example, that almost all universities, public and private, are 501(c)(3) organizations, and presidents of universities, admittedly a demanding job, commonly earn seven-figure salaries. In the case of a successful tier 2 pay-to-play sports club, likely the director, who may well have established the club, is making six figures from a combination of a salary for administering the club, additional salary from coaching one or more teams, and further income from sources such as organizing a tournament (if the director is listed as the vendor for that tournament, then all profit from the tournament goes to him or her), and private tutorial sessions with players.

Team coaches at tier 2 clubs make roughly between $8,000 and $15,000, depending in part on which area of the country the club is located and the local cost of living, for each team they coach. In practice, the business models of many pay-to-play youth-sports clubs increasingly resemble the gig economy, with just a very few at the top making a lot of money and everyone else not so much. But few coaches at tier 2 clubs try to make a full-time living from coaching. More likely, the salary from coaching and perhaps tutoring and other ancillary activities is a healthy supplement to the income from another job. If a tier 2 club is content with its tier 2 status, which can provide a healthy revenue stream by casting a wide net, then the pressure on coaches from club administrators to win may be somewhat muted. But the situation could be quite the opposite for the coaches if the tier 2 club is seeking to move up to tier 1 status, as difficult an endeavor in the youth-sports market as it can be to advance one's position in just about any other competitive market in the United States.

Location looms large in whether a club can ever rise to the status of tier 1. If there is not a sufficient population base to guarantee a large pool of players, the most talented of which eventually gravitate to one or two local tier 1 clubs, it is extraordinarily difficult for a club to elevate itself to tier 1 status and maintain that status. Statistically, it is next to impossible for a club drawing from a small population base to compete nationally year after year, however talented the coaching staff might be. There may be the occasional great team, the statistical aberration that emerges, but that is rare.

Even in Portland, Oregon, which likes to think of itself as Soccer City USA, an honest appraisal of the situation would conclude that in 2021 none of the clubs were tier 1. In terms of population, Portland is the 26th largest city in the United States. If there were one club that had truly managed to distinguish itself from all the other clubs, thus attracting almost all of the top players, it might be possible for Portland to be home to one tier 1 pay-to-play soccer club. It is also possible to imagine it being home to one tier 1 club each for boys and for girls. But this is not the case, and the population base is simply not sufficient for any of the clubs to compete year in, year out, with clubs from Seattle, Southern California, New York City, and other major population centers. Consequently, profitmaking from youth sports in sparsely populated Oregon pales in comparison to more-populated areas.

There have been a few legendary club teams in Portland's youth-soccer history, including a few club national champions. But as a general rule, Portland-based club teams are competitive with but lose more often than they win against Seattle-based club teams (the population of the Seattle metropolitan area is about twice that of Portland). The situation can be far more unequal when Portland teams go up against those based in the major metropolitan areas in California. Needless to say, it is even less likely that clubs in areas with smaller populations than Portland could ever achieve and maintain tier 1 status, although they may produce some excellent players. Unsurprisingly, the Portland-based clubs tend to beat up on the clubs based throughout the rest of Oregon. But the attraction of tier 1 clubs results in the phenomenon of some families undertaking, regularly, Herculean commutes so that a young athlete can play for a tier 1 club team. We know of several cases of families from rural Oregon making regular six-hour round-trip commutes to practices and games in Portland and also of several Portland families who switched to clubs in Seattle and thereafter made the regular six-hour round-trip commute for practices and games. Some elite clubs have practices four times per week, each adding up to a full day of commuting.

For the simple reason that there are only so many nexuses of population density, tier 2 and tier 3 clubs are far more common than tier 1 clubs. Tier 3 clubs would likely not be taken seriously if they attached the elite label to themselves, but that does not mean that they cannot be successful financially. At the tier 3 level, player fees will constitute almost all of the revenue. But large numbers of players, even from families paying less of a fee than would be the case at the higher-level clubs, can still add up to significant revenue that often considerably exceeds expenses.

One of the many surprising aspects of pay-to-play sports is that more parents do not avail themselves of the fact that the annual tax filings of nonprofit organizations are public domain, providing a window into how the clubs are doing financially and where the money is going. Many parents would likely be surprised to learn that the club director makes more than they do. Perhaps this side of pay-to-play sports is why almost no pay-to-play clubs provide their members with accounting of the finances of the nonprofit. One option that families should consider is insisting on a full public accounting of these finances. Since they are nonprofits, much but not all of the information is accessible through an online search, and parents could insist that all financial information be provided to the families annually without having to search for it.

Tournaments that give large numbers of teams a chance to play, whatever the level of competition, can still be quite profitable. Even a director who is managing a club almost individually, perhaps with volunteer help from some parents, is likely working long hours. All the more so if the director has ambitions of moving the club up the hierarchy. Booking sufficient field space for practices and other activities can be a major challenge and is fiercely competitive. For this reason, wealthier clubs often build their own field complexes. But scheduling is still a complex logistical operation. Tournaments do not run themselves. Organizing and running a tournament potentially represents a few months of pure insanity for the club director or directors, lucrative though they can be. Even at the tier 3 level, profits can range between $50,000 and $75,000.

But those amounts are paltry compared to what some famous tournaments generate. Although the numbers are not public, individuals with inside knowledge believe that several tournaments or combinations of tournaments likely net clubs more than $1 million annually. These include the Target USA Cup in Minnesota (its website bills it as the "greatest soccer experience in the world with 1,200-plus teams together to open up the tournament"), the various tournaments sponsored by North Carolina FC, the Surf Cup tournaments in San Diego, California, the Jefferson Cup held in Richmond, Virginia, and those sponsored by the Scott Gallagher St. Louis Soccer Club in Missouri. In short, tournaments have become big business and not just for soccer but for many youth sports.

Coaches at tier 3 clubs make less, but it is still a chance for someone to supplement income through coaching that did not exist forty years ago. At $5,000 to $8,000 per team for a head coach, the supplemental income can be meaningful. It is far less likely that the coach will be expected to travel repeatedly for distant tournaments, as is the case with coaches for tier 1 clubs, who may travel as many as ten to fifteen long weekends per year for competitions, making their positions far more demanding than those of tier 2 and tier 3 coaches. Tier 3 coaches also may not be expected to win.

How does a club attract players? For tier 1 clubs, reputation alone usually takes care of that. Families will find them. For clubs in tier 2 and tier 3, in addition to a strong web presence, old-fashioned marketing (e.g., signs at busy intersections) is employed. One of the best ways to attract players is to convince elementary schools to allow the club to distribute literature about the sports opportunities offered by the club, especially if practices take place nearby. Every player is revenue so best to get them early. Simple inertia will keep many families in the same club if the club can sign them up when the kids begin playing a sport.

It is not unusual for professional players, after retirement, to establish clubs that are based on the prestige they earned while playing professionally. This prestige can help a former professional get a club up and running and attract players and also attract a large number of summer campers but only for as long as the former professional player's name carries cachet. A new generation of parents may not be familiar with the former professional, who was once a respected member of the local professional team but hardly a superstar whose fame transcends generations. If a club whose initial success was largely predicated on the name power of one individual does not develop significant infrastructure, including in the area of marketing, it may end up failing.

There is a never-ending flow of retiring professional players faced with the "what next?" question, and newly retired athletes may have more cachet than their aging counterparts. Many of the rules that apply to for-profit businesses apply to the nonprofit sector, including youth sports. Market entry is by no means easy since many pay-to-play markets are already saturated. Often several clubs in any given metropolitan area have established a de facto oligopoly and do not take kindly to ambitious newcomers seeking to claim a piece of the pie. A few youth-sports markets, such as lacrosse, are in the growth phase, or emerging-market stage, to use a business-sector term. But participation in most other youth sports is declining, static, or growing only slightly, resulting in intensely competitive markets.

The clubs and the various leagues are the most important pieces of the increasingly large puzzle that includes so many agents involved in the Youth Sports Industry. Connecting the various dots is crucial to understanding why Americans spend $20 billion on youth sports. Arguably, the most important part of the overall ecosystem that explains pay-to-play youth sports in the United States is college sports, the practice of preferential admission to athletes and in some cases scholarships. That college sports looms so large in youth sports is evidenced not only by the emphasis that clubs and leagues put on their role as being able to place their players on college teams but also by the number of ancillary businesses that exist to assist in this process.

The College Admissions Race

The odds are stacked against the athletically average kid ever playing in college no matter how much money is invested in coaching that child in a sport. Nonetheless, there are sufficient numbers of families endeavoring to claim spots on college teams that parents not only pay for club fees and travel but also to contract with ancillary businesses to assist with the college-search process to help with securing a spot on a college team. For the rare young athlete who has been identified as junior-national-teams level, receiving multiple offers from college is a given. For soccer, there are perhaps thirty young men and thirty young women who constitute the junior-national-teams pool. Although the families of these rare athletes have likely spent tens of thousands, perhaps even hundreds of thousands of dollars, along the way on pay-to-play sports, the college search should largely take care of itself.

Junior-national-team-level players are hot commodities, and coaches will find such players. These players will receive offers of athletic scholarships, whether or not their families require assistance for their child to receive a college education. This is a curious anomaly for the one sector of American society, higher education, that otherwise requires families to pay what they can afford rather than a set fee, through financial-aid programs. Well-to-do families are required to pay full price, unless their child has an athletic scholarship.

For players who are not in the junior-national-team pool to play in college, it will likely be necessary to go the extra mile to attract the attention of college coaches. Or extra thousands of miles, literally. The problem is compounded by the difficulty of finding a spot on a team at a college that is also a good match academically, socially, and perhaps in terms of location. How does a youth athlete attract the attention of college coaches? It is increasingly common that youth athletes must jump through a remarkable series of hoops, often expensive hoops, to get the attention of coaches.

As players reach high-school age or even earlier in some cases, the main justification for tournaments is that they provide a venue to be seen by college coaches. An expensive endeavor, it may take attendance at several showcase tournaments (coaches often do not travel to showcases beyond their regions) to attract attention from even one coach. The explosion of showcase tournaments, with as many as four major showcase tournaments going on during any given weekend, has created a tremendous dilution of the number of college coaches who can attend any given showcase. This has led some organizers of showcase tournaments to engage in practices bordering on fraud, including listing as participating coaches those who will supposedly watch video of the tournament games.

Meanwhile, college coaches themselves have wised up to the amount of money that families will pay to be "seen" and increasingly they undercut showcase tournaments by insisting that prospective players attend one or more of their ID camps. Showcase tournaments predated ID camps, but eventually college coaches realized the financial and convenience benefits of gathering prospective players, for a fee of course, at their campus or at nearby facilities with the hook that those players catching the eye of the coaching staff might get a spot on their college team. The fact that ID camps are now cutting into the value of showcase tournaments has in turn led some pay-to-play leagues to fight back. The MLS Next Rules & Regulations 2020–2021 includes limits and regulations regarding MLS Next players attending college camps. MLS Next defines as part of its mission providing "a professional player development and an elite development pathway for future college players," so it is important that MLS Next's own showcase tournaments maintain their relevance in the college-recruitment process.

Getting the attention of a college coach is not easy in no small part because so many youth athletes are trying to do just that. Families are aware of the level of competition, and one of the peculiarities of the tournament experience for youth athletes who are hoping to play at the college level is that they may spend hours in advance of the tournament sending out as many as 100 emails to coaches who are advertised as being expected to attend. Coaches are so deluged with these emails that they often cannot possibly read all that arrive, much less reply to them. Often the only reply that a youth athlete will receive is an auto-reply directing them to attend an ID camp. Even if a coach takes the time to watch a particular player, it is typically for only about twenty minutes, and rarely does that serve to convince the coach.

The recruiting game is a complex dance involving various steps. The path to a place on a college team often involves an all-out campaign frequently requiring parents to reach for a credit card to get coaches to sign their dance card to have their child evaluated. Even after having seen a player in action at one tournament, coaches, unless they are already a hard no or a fast yes about a player, will typically require numerous additional dances. Coaches are typically in no hurry to sign players in the middle-mass group that can play at the college level but are not seen as "game-changers," and they have many ways of putting off the decision. In the meantime, the coach might attract more star players so best to keep the options open for as long as possible.

Coaches are not in agreement about the value of footage. Some rely on it a great deal, and footage took on particular importance during the pandemic. But other coaches, even during normal times, refuse to base their decisions on footage. Those coaches who do value footage value different types of footage. Some want to see one half from one match in which the player performed well while other coaches want to see a highlight reel. Self-producing a compilation of playing footage is less expensive than contracting this to a professional, but it still requires the purchase of some sort of filming device and tripod that will produce a quality of footage that will be meaningful.

There are also many services that will film multiple games for a team for a fee. It is almost always the case that every team attending a competitive tournament receives an offer from a company specializing in the filming of youth-sports games. Participation in showcase tournaments often involves players completing online profiles that require their email addresses and often the email addresses of their parents, ostensibly so that coaches can conveniently contact them. The part of this dance that grows tiresome is that the tournaments promptly share these email addresses, presumably for a fee, with a variety of commercial enterprises.

The offer to film a team's games typically involves filming all of the team's group-round games for a set price that averages out, at minimum, to about $200 per game, with the suggestion that the parents share the set fee in return for all receiving the footage. This is sometimes a good way to have footage of a game in which a parents' young athlete was "in the zone," playing as well as he or she has ever played, and that might be enough to catch the attention of a college coach. But for those coaches who prefer highlight reels, there is still the necessary step of copying and pasting short clips from numerous games into a compilation. Done by outside contractors, the price of the final product can easily reach $2,000.

There are also companies that will livestream games so those who could not attend can watch it, making livestreaming of youth-sports games a market niche. The footage can also be later submitted, perhaps in edited form, to college coaches. The price to have a game livestreamed and also archived is similar to the cost of conventional filming.

The more families that are willing to go in for such a service, the less cost to each family. There is also the emerging area of video analysis, companies that not only livestream games for teams but that also provide software that allows for sophisticated analysis of what a team did well and areas for improvement.

Before pandemic conditions, footage alone was almost never sufficient for a college coach to offer a youth athlete a spot. Coaches might say that they must see a player at additional tournaments before making a decision. Or that the player must attend one of their ID camps.

One of the contradictions of the Youth Sports Industry especially evident in the area of soccer but largely true of other sports as well, is that the key marketing tool of elite leagues such as ECNL and MLS Next is the presence of college coaches at their events, but increasingly college coaches simply tell interested players to attend one of their ID camps. Basically, multiple entities are trying to claw money from families hoping to facilitate their child getting a spot on a college team. What compounds the system is that whether or not a player gets a place on a college team sometimes boils down to connections more so than merit, the willingness of a club coach to call in a favor from an old friend who is now coaching a college team, for example.

Coaches advertise ID camps widely, but they are well aware, ahead of time in many cases, that most to even all of the players attending are of no interest. But coaches seem happy to take their camp fees nonetheless, and a single program may host 150 players for a one-day camp. It is also common for multiple programs to come together to host an ID camp, and with more coaches in attendance the upper limit for participating players can be increased. The Atlantic ID Camp held in Bel Air, Maryland, in July of 2021 attracted more than 375 boys.

ID camps are typically held at the facilities of the college or nearby. The fee for the camp varies in its duration, but as a basic rule a camp that lasts one day typically costs $250 to $300, with each additional day adding about $100 to the overall cost. Coaches at academically elite colleges such as Ivy League schools often can charge more. Many camps are only one day in length. If the college happens to be nearby, at least within driving distance, the registration fee represents most of the cost of attendance.

But it is common for players to fly to these camps, often with an accompanying adult depending on the player's age. Add on to the cost of air travel whether a rental car will be necessary to get from the airport to the camp and often at least one night in a nearby hotel because it is not possible to arrive by plane in the morning of a camp and then fly out that same evening. This can easily push the cost of attending even a single ID camp toward $1,000. And it is not unusual for a coach to insist that a prospect attend a second, third, or even fourth ID camp, with a corresponding compounding of the overall cost. And that is just for one college program, which may not pan out in the end.

When our second daughter attended some ID camps in between her sophomore and junior year (Full disclosure: She played for the soccer and lacrosse teams at an excellent and ethically grounded DIII program as the result of her experience at one of these ID camps, so there are success stories), we talked with other parents. More than one parent explained how his or her daughter was basically spending the entire summer going from one ID camp to another without any bites whatsoever from coaches.

But it would be simplistic to blame the college coaches. What exactly were the parents and the players thinking? A dose of self-reflection would undoubtedly serve many parents and players alike. Our second daughter, while helping out at a soccer ID camp at her DIII school, encountered a father, who, after accosting her, grilled her on exactly which classes she had taken in high school that facilitated admission to the college she attends, generally considered one of the elite ones. He seemed to believe that there was some secret formula and if he could just fathom the secret then the holy grail of admission could be achieved.

The dream of a spot on a college team dies hard, even though it may be totally unrealistic. If a pay-to-play club coach gives parents an honest appraisal of the unlikelihood of their child playing at the college level, the family may then storm off to another club. Such behavior hardly encourages coaches to try to head off parents chasing fantasies by offering thoughtful appraisals of a child's lack of potential to play at the college level.

Of course such evaluations can be subjective although in many cases there is unanimity, so obvious it is that the player is unsuited for the college level. Still, a certain level of skepticism on the part of the family leads them to seek a second opinion. Incredible though it may seem, some pay-to-play youth-sports coaches are having their back scratched by a particular family and may be pushing that family's player whether or not the player's ability justifies such attention. But when multiple coaches are offering the same evaluation, it is time to face reality.

Despite the fact that attending multiple distant ID camps is only available to families in the upper 5 or 10 percent of the socioeconomic elite, in rare cases there may be a democratic element to the ID-camp system. There is always the chance that a player from afar who the coach otherwise never would have seen play can make such an impression on a coach during an ID camp that the player can earn a position on the team. But this possibility assumes that the family can cover all of the attendant costs, so just how democratic is it?

For the socioeconomic elite for whom resources are not a problem, there is an almost endless array of ancillary businesses offering for-fee services to help gain admission to college not just for student athletes but for students in general. Families can contract with a prospective college-athlete recruitment consulting service, which has become a big business. As of 2020, Next Student College Athlete, one of the larger recruiting services, employed 400-plus recruiting coordinators and recruiting specialists—terms and professions that did not exist a generation ago for transitioning high-school student-athletes to college-sports programs—and a total of 800 employees. Its annual revenues are in the range of $60 million.

NCSA is only one of many such services. How much do such services cost, and what do they do? The cost question is actually not as easy to answer as one might hope because almost none of these agencies post prices for their various packages on their websites. Requiring the consumer to play a game of cat-and-mouse about price is typically a red flag regarding how a business operates, whatever the sector. Typically, one has to fill out a form providing information on the player who is seeking consultation services, which typically results in a request for a phone appointment for a representative to give the pitch.

So, for the purposes of this book, we called one of them to inquire about our son. The gentleman on the other end of the phone employed a typical sales strategy of hope and fear—if you partner with us, there is great promise for your son; if you do not partner with us, well, best not to think about the consequences. A discount was offered if we agreed right then and there to the expensive package. It was a classic demonstration of sales tactics, carefully pitched in this case to play on the fear of parents that they are not doing everything humanly possible to help their child to succeed in an age of hyper competition. Our then 15-year-old son, who was on the call, was even more disgusted than we were.

The typical college-athlete-recruitment consultancy company generally offers about four levels of packages. These range from several hundred dollars for the most basic package, for which one receives a one-hour phone consultation with a recruiting specialist (who will try to upsell the family to a higher level of service) to more than $3,000, which can be due annually for MVP-level service. This is a service only for those who have ample resources or for those who are desperate to do whatever it takes to get their child a spot on a college team.

Most everyone who has taken a critical look at college-athlete recruitment consultants would not call the more reputable organizations outright scams. For families with money to burn that want someone else to help guide their child through what admittedly can be a time-consuming process, they may be convenient. But they can rightly be considered part of an overall trend toward disempowering the young student athlete, who if motivated to play in college will not need such a helping hand. Consultancies have databases of all the college-sports programs in the country along with the emails of the coaching staff, but this information is also available online at the athletics pages of the college websites. NCSA and other consultancies provide a matching service by which the player provides athletic and academic input and then is provided a list of good matching colleges. But any seasoned and honest club coach should be able to inform a player of what level of college sports the player is capable of achieving. Any college's website in general provides information on what constitutes an academic match.

All of the college coaches we contacted or spoke with scoffed at these sorts of consulting services, saying that they played no meaningful role in their recruiting decisions, but the websites of these agencies include testimonials from college coaches about their value and relevance. Were these paid endorsements?

There are so many other agents involved in the Youth Sports Industry. Next we turn our attention to the tournament circuit.

Chapter 3

Tournacations

What Purpose Do They Serve and at What Cost?

When queried about the developmental value of tournaments requiring significant travel and expense, youth-sports coaches offered passionate opinions that tournaments have either no or next to no developmental value, especially at the younger ages. There was a unanimity of opinion that even if they played a minuscule role in helping kids develop into better soccer, basketball, or hockey players, the return in terms of development was so small compared to the expense that there was no justification for tournaments that require overnight stays. Almost all tournaments operate with essentially no oversight other than by the organizer, which is to say that they operate with no oversight from governing sports bodies, governmental bodies, or other entities that might rein in the excesses of the tournament circuit.

The consensus about the lack of developmental value at the younger ages was especially resounding, so much so that coaches scoffed at the tournament circuit. While at the United States Youth Soccer's Far West Regional Tournament in 2021, we happened upon a U-13 boys game. Within a minute or two, one of the early developers breezed by opponents a foot shorter and scored a goal. Did it provide any indication of where he and all the others on the field would be six years from now? Developmentally, the presence of teams at this age at a regional tournament is largely a waste of time and money. So why does United States Youth Soccer continue this practice?

What purposes do tournaments serve? There are many outcomes, but most are divorced from player development. Many kids love tournaments. For the right type of kid, it is close to a dream come true to travel, often by plane, with peers to a new place, stay in a luxurious hotel with teammates (typically sharing a room with three others), eat meals at restaurants, and play sports matches. Additional and more important purposes for why tournaments have become so prominent include economic return for clubs and all the other entities that dip into the lucrative tournament trough, parental egos that celebrate the raising of a trophy by their child, and parents who frankly enjoy the excuse for a vacation that a tournament provides—a "tournacation." At the older ages, when tournaments begin to have some developmental purpose, they are often justified as a means for players to be seen and hopefully recruited by college coaches. Thus the term "showcase tournament." But showcase tournaments themselves often do not live up to their billing, calling into question the value of the entire tournament circuit.

Some simple arithmetic will help to better explain why serious coaches interested in developing the skills of young players scorn tournaments. Consider the following scenario. A U-11 team from Portland, Oregon, is set to attend a tournament in San Diego, California. Let's pencil out the per-family costs involved. Tournament fees are $1,200 per team, so that is $75 per family if we assume sixteen players. The airfare will be in the range of $400 to $500. But few parents will send a 10-to-11-year-old child alone—and in many cases clubs will require an accompanying parent—so double the cost of the airfare. Additionally, the families must pay not only the cost of the plane tickets but also the lodging and meal costs of the coaches, which adds up to about $100 per family.

Each family will need its own room at one of the hotels at which teams are required to stay, and they are far from budget hotels. The room cost for the parent will typically be at least $220 per night, times three nights, so $660. At the United States Youth Soccer's Far West Regionals in Boise, Idaho, as a result of our son's U-18 club team having won the Oregon State Cup, the Hampton Inn, an official tournament hotel, was pleasant enough, and yet the rate was $225 per night, so $225 for our room, and $225 divided four ways for our son's room shared with teammates.

It is unusual for the hotels to be within walking distance of the playing fields, so typically a rental car is also required for those who fly. Some teams rent vans and split the cost. Other families join forces to share a budget rental, so, conservatively, let's say $100 for three days in San Diego. There is also the cost of food. Breakfast is probably included with the lodging, so, including meals at airports, food costs for parent and child can run to $140 or more. This does not include the $30 T-shirt commemorating participation in the tournament, or the fact that keeping a bunch of 10- and 11-year olds from destroying hotel beds with jumping games often requires an outing to a water park or arcade. The total per family is $1,975 and could easily be more.

The amount would be the same for just about any sports team from Oregon going to a tournament in San Diego. But let's continue with the calculations based on it being a soccer tournament. At the typical soccer tournament, a U-11 team is guaranteed three games no longer than 60 minutes in length, although the games may in fact be shorter. If the team advances to the championship game, it will play a total of five games. So the team, which typically includes five to six more players than can be on the field at any given time, plays somewhere between 180 and 300 minutes of soccer.

If the team gets only the minimum 180 minutes of game time (at many tournaments, if the team does not advance out of group stage there are no additional consolation matches), the cost per minute of playing time per player is just under $11. But since most players will only play about two-thirds of the overall 180 minutes, the cost actually rises to about $16.45 per minute, or $987 per hour of playing time. If the team advances to the championship game and each player gets 200 minutes out of a total of 300 minutes of playing time, the cost per minute of playing time declines to a little over $9.85, or $592.50 per hour. Few families would pay $987 or even $592 per hour for anything else other than perhaps medical care, and yet this is what they are paying per hour for their child's playing time at tournaments.

Doing the arithmetic helps better understand why coaches who are interested in developing better soccer players dismiss tournaments as meaningless extravaganzas but also why parents are known to measure precisely with stopwatches how many minutes of playing time their child receives. Nonetheless, it is an eerie feeling to be at a youth-sports match and notice that when a round of subs enters the game, nearby parents start their stopwatches (no doubt the coach will hear later if there were any suspicious imbalances). But all this has nothing to do with developing better soccer players, returning us to the puzzling question of why tournaments became such a feature of pay-to-play youth soccer and sports in general. Plain and simple, it is because they make some people quite a lot of money, but there is also a broader culture of tournaments involving prestige and status.

When our second daughter was playing U-12 soccer for a club in one of the suburbs of Portland, Oregon, we were informed by the coach of his intention to take the team to Las Vegas for a tournament, which would require flying and three nights in a hotel. Although this suburb of Portland is wealthy, some of the parents were not convinced of the necessity of such a trip, which was going to cost each family in the range of $1,500 if a parent accompanied the player. The parents did the unthinkable in the context of pay-to-play youth sports—they demanded that the coach explain the reasoning behind it. At this point the coach, who far from being a monster was on balance one of the better coaches our two daughters had over the years, made a revealing mistake. He repeated a line that he must have been using for years to justify travel to these sorts of tournaments, announcing that "we need to find competition."

But the problem with this line of reasoning in reference to this particular team was that the team had finished fifth in the league that comprised Oregon pay-to-play club teams at that age, suggesting that they were in no need whatsoever of travel to find competition. They clearly faced plenty of competition within Oregon. And so it went back and forth for a while between a minority of skeptical parents and the coach, who had in his hand an ace card, which he played. He made it abundantly clear that by goodness the team was going, and if any individual player did not go the spot would be offered to a player on the U-11 team. With a large reserve of families eager to be able to tell neighbors, friends, and relatives that their U-11 daughter was "playing up" on the U-12 team for a tournament in Las Vegas, the coach had the stronger hand. This was true in spite of the fact that the selection of U-11 players had almost entirely to do with the family's ability to pay rather than the daughter's skills as a soccer player.

As part of this process, the coach did admit that the real reason he was so desperate to take the U-12 team to this tournament was because "if we don't go to their tournament, they won't come to ours." And so the truth began to emerge. The Nike Tournament that this particular club sponsored was a big moneymaker, so much so that the coach's livelihood was in part dependent on it. This particular coach was not a part-time coach. His full-time job was coaching for and helping to manage the club. The reason for this U-12 team's participation in the Las Vegas tournament had virtually nothing to do with "finding competition" or player development and everything to do with the families further subsidizing the club, beyond the basic annual fees in the range of $2,000. It was an indirect subsidy in the sense that by attending this Las Vegas tournament, the Las Vegas team, as well as many other teams, would come to our club's tournament, thus enriching our club's coffers.

Typically, the more prestigious a tournament (the most-prestigious tournaments tend to be sponsored by famous clubs), the greater the revenue. Prestige for older ages often derives from being able to advertise mass attendance by college coaches, even if the chance is small that one's child's team may end up with a game on the so-called "right field" where college coaches scout for any length of time. There is no codified definition of what it means for a college coach to "attend" a tournament, so stopping by for fifteen minutes could be advertised as attending. Of course, large tournaments, whatever the level of competition, can also be lucrative.

This was more the case with the tournament our daughter's coach was concerned about—maximizing participation in a tournament sponsored by his club. The profit from tournaments comes not only from registration fees, minus the costs of field rentals, referees, and other expenses, but also from sponsorships, concessions, parking, and partnering fees from hotels. One run-of-the-mill yet successful tournament, meaning the tournament attracted teams mostly regionally with maybe a few teams flying in to participate, can shore up a club's bank account for an entire year, garnering upwards of $50,000 to $100,000. But that is pocket change compared to what is netted by Surf Cups, tournaments sponsored by North Carolina FC, and the various tournaments that take place at the ESPN Wide World of Sports Complex in Orlando, Florida, which is owned by Disney. Unsurprisingly, with the numerous attractions available close at hand, tournaments that take place at the ESPN Wide World of Sports Complex represent the quintessential tournacation.

Our daughter did not want to be left out of going to Las Vegas with her team, and we could afford it, sort of, so we sent her accompanied by her mother, which was appropriate for that age, especially because with celiac disease our daughter needed to eat gluten free, not easy territory for an 11-year old to navigate away from home. But this was a turning point for us when it came to conceptualizing tournaments. Suspicions had emerged that would only grow in the coming years. It was during our daughter's time in Las Vegas that we first learned that the club organizing the tournament, which requires participating teams to stay in designated hotels, receives what in old-fashioned terms is known as "kickbacks" from the hotels. The kickbacks are often in the form of free hotel rooms that the organizers can use to lodge referees and especially college coaches in order to entice them to come to a tournament so that their presence can be leveraged to get teams to register in the first place. This explained the requirement that the teams stay only in hotels designated by the tournament.

However much our kids loved these tournaments—and many parents loved them, too, gathering at the bar when the kids were in bed—it had become clear to us that they had very little to do with developing players and much to do with extracting money from those families who could afford it. There was also quite an economic burden on those families who, depending on one's definition of "affording it" (e.g., having to forego contributions to the retirement account), probably could not afford it but felt the pressure to comply. Considering its previous performance in Oregon, it was no surprise that our daughter's team did not make the playoffs at the Las Vegas tournament, which is known as three and done. The team played three games and that was the end of the tournament for the girls—three and done. So, for a total of $24,000 (16 families shelling out an average of $1,500 each), the team got 180 minutes of soccer. Returning to the arithmetic, since most kids only played two-thirds or 120 minutes of soccer, this came out to $12.50 per minute, or $750 per hour, of playing time per player. If facing the "competition" in Las Vegas led to any improvement in their performance, it seemed lost on the parents. The team continued to struggle against the local pay-to-play teams, no different than before the economic outlay for the weekend trip to Las Vegas.

We did, during many years of pay-to-play soccer, experience one coach who took a more thoughtful view of what was developmentally useful. For our son's U-12 team, which was flush with talent, the coach nonetheless announced that spending money was not high on his list and that there was no particular need to go to tournaments requiring travel by plane. What made this announcement all the more powerful was that this coach was once a star for the local professional soccer team, the Portland Timbers, with his number retired as part of the Ring of Honor. Additionally, no soccer coach in Oregon had nurtured more players who went on to play professional soccer than he had, suggesting that he knew as much as anyone in Oregon about developing soccer players.

The Selection Process and Family Dynamics

The typical process by which players are selected to play in a tournament often contributes to the decision-making by the family about whether or not to send a child. There are certainly clubs that lay out at the beginning of the season the expectations about participation in tournaments and the likely costs. With elite clubs that attend numerous tournaments, the costs per child of participating in pay-to-play can be as high as $30,000 annually. Other clubs do not explicitly lay out the expected costs at the beginning of the season, leading to many surprises for parents along the way. Additionally, a certain percentage of teams employ the "pool system." This means that there is a group of what are referred to as "swing players," players who are ranked as being in the no man's land between the first and second teams.

This can be a stressful situation. Clubs portray it as providing a useful competitive cauldron (if players improve during the course of the year, they can move up to the first team; players on the first team who slack off can also be demoted) that nurtures development, but we have our doubts. It is not clear that it is in fact a system that creates more benefit than it does harm. It leaves certain kids endlessly hoping that they get the call up to the first team. Additionally, it helps clubs keep families in line in terms of selection for tournaments, which is perhaps why some clubs employ it.

For clubs using the pool system, the manager or coach indicates that on such and such day—often surprisingly close to the tournament—the roster for the tournament that the first team is attending will be unveiled (second teams also go to tournaments but often not ones with the same level of prestige). Families of the better players on the team can assume that their child will be selected and plan accordingly. If money is not an issue, they can choose to send their child even if they understand that the tournament is mostly a vacation rather than part of the developmental process.

It is the families from which the truly gifted players come who have the most leverage. Everybody wants such players, so these families are in the best position to decline the endless tournament circuit and other demands by coaches that have far more to do with the needs of the clubs and coaches than what is in the best interest of the player. Whatever disappointment or threats the coach might express are hollow. There will always be a spot on a team for the game-changing player who helps win matches. And so long as the player loves the sport and thus naturally wants to excel, that player will reach full potential regardless of tournaments attended or declined.

Difficult though it is for some parents to accept, to a considerable extent talent in sports is predetermined, although judgment must be reserved at the younger ages. For the rare player who is on track to play in college or even at a higher level, missed tournaments are not going to change that trajectory. Along the same lines, for players who are not destined to play in college, participation in yet another tournament is not going to make a difference.

But this is not so easy to keep in mind if one's son or daughter is a so-called swing player who has been selected to accompany the first team to a tournament. At first glance, it can seem as though validation has come at long last. The player has earned a spot on the first team going forward. And in some cases that is true. But more often than not, the situation is more ambiguous. Maybe some of the better players on the first team are injured or have indicated their unavailability for other reasons. But by goodness the team is going to the tournament. So the coach will fill out the roster by whatever means necessary. Typically there are no promises that a swing player selected will get equal or even much playing time.

For clubs trying to achieve and maintain the highest level of elite status, the only way to get invited to truly prestigious tournaments is to attend medium-level tournaments and hopefully perform well enough there. Attendance at the most prestigious tournaments (e.g., Surf Cup) provides marketing leverage for the club to attract more players.

A certain drama is connected to the announcement of the players who have been selected for the tournament. The roster will be sent out by email or posted on the likes of Teamsnap, a sports management app that allows for efficient online communication. For some kids, joy or tears will follow. This is a normal part of life, but until this generation of youth athletes a positive result in athletics did not typically include a significant price tag for the parents. Try telling a swing-player child who has finally been offered a spot on the first team, even just for a long weekend, that it does not fit in the family's plans. Aside from the money, those not yet initiated into pay-to-play sports may be surprised at how late these invitations to tournaments can come. They can arrive two weeks or even less before the team will fly off to the tournament.

This time frame is possible because the club will have already purchased the requisite number of plane tickets through a travel agency that specializes in youth-sports travel, and they will subsequently attach player names to those tickets, with payment then coming from the families. But what if the tournament conflicts with a long-planned family vacation that the parents managed to schedule with considerable difficulty?

There are legitimate feelings to be addressed. If selected, a swing player finally feels accepted and wants to seize the opportunity to prove that he or she belongs on the first team going forward. But there is also a fear factor, often promoted by clubs and coaches, that can derail rational decision-making. The club or coach hints that a refusal to accept the invitation to this tournament will influence the selection of rosters for future tournaments. (It is astonishing that pay-to-play coaches have come to assume that every family is prepared to drop $2,000 for a tournament on short notice as though that were the most normal thing in the world.) Even if the club or coach does not play dirty and make such threats about future decisions, the overall anxiety of the situation can lead player and parents alike wondering if they must seize this opportunity now to ensure that there will be future opportunities.

The answer to that question is somewhere in the range of "it depends" to "no." If the family vacation is not being affected, money is not a concern, and the parents are aware that the tournaments play next to no role in sports development, although they can loom large in terms of socialization and developing a peer group, then the decision to let one's child attend, so long as it is not driven by fear, is fine. But if the family is so worried that a refusal might lead to a coach pointedly not selecting the player in the future, then perhaps the question should be, "Why are we part of this club and why are we working with such a coach?"

If a club or coach backs up selections with fear-mongering about future decisions, does the club or coach really value a player as a human being? Or are they simply trying to gauge which family is wealthy or desperate enough to immediately accept such invitations, thus quickening the process by which the coach fills out roster spots fourteen, fifteen, sixteen, and maybe seventeen for a team traveling to a tournament? Once a club and a coach have decided to take a team to a tournament, they will insist on filling the roster by whatever means are at their disposal.

In the end, it will often come down to who is willing to pay more rather than who deserves to be on the roster. Once a coach has filled the roster, final travel arrangements must be made. We became aware of what a financial stretch some of these tournaments are for many families through experiencing the strategies clubs have developed to extract payment. In almost every case when one of our child's teams went to a tournament that required plane travel, a message would go out warning that under no circumstances would a player be provided with a plane ticket until payment for the tournament or at least the plane ticket had been received by the club. Promise of payment meant nothing. The check or credit card needed to be received and processed. Obviously the club had been burned enough times previously that it now required upfront payment. And clubs are not above distributing the amount of unpaid bills of team members along to the remaining families to absorb!

Then the team manager will send out either hard figures or estimates of all the additional costs. Additionally, the team manager is more or less expected not only to book a sufficient number of rooms for the players, coaches, and team manager but also to get the hotel to set aside a block of rooms for parents who also want to attend the tournament, to be individually reserved by parents by a specific deadline. When our first daughter was little, her mother would more often than not accompany her and also took on various volunteer tasks (e.g., driving some of the players to and from the games). She was always amazed to see some parents who were using the tournament as an excuse for a vacation but who showed up only at games, leaving all the tasks of taking care of a group of preteens to other parents. This drives home what these tournaments mean to some parents, namely a wonderful excuse to ditch parenting for a long weekend except for the excitement of the games.

But there is also the other side of the coin involving financially stretched families. Most clubs provide some sort of financial aid to allow especially talented kids from families who could otherwise not participate in pay-to-play sports, but this rarely extends to the cost of travel tournaments. This is more than a little ironic considering the importance with which clubs portray tournaments. If the clubs truly considered tournaments that important to development, presumably financial aid would extend to these costs. But tournaments are so expensive that they would likely burn through the financial-aid budget.

We have seen players at tournaments who were sent solo with either no or grossly insufficient funds for meals, frequently the one tournament cost for which payment is not required in advance. This led to awkward, likely humiliating moments for the player, until some parent with a heart or deep pocketbook or both stepped up to make sure that the player got decent meals during the tournament. Our anger was directed not at the parents of these players, who were no doubt doing their best, but rather at the clubs. Such players were often among the best on the team, selected because they helped the team win. The clubs and coaches were perfectly well aware of the financial situation of the parents and yet took no action to make sure meals would be covered. They just assumed that one or more of the parents would take care of the matter, a correct assumption under the untenable situation that would develop during mealtimes and one that left a preteen not knowing how he or she was going to eat and then having to accept a handout.

Travel and Loads of Dead Time

In the two weeks leading up to a tournament, especially the larger ones, families of participating players will receive, in addition to instructions about how the player can market himself or herself to college coaches, various commercial solicitations. Would the team like to commemorate its participation in the tournament by getting a special team T-shirt made? And so on. Since the wealthy are disproportionately represented in pay-to-play sports, it is perhaps only natural that various vendors hope to realize a profit from those participating in these tournaments.

One purpose that travel tournaments can serve is to make experienced travelers out of kids. But the tournament travel process also includes a lot of time spent doing nothing particularly useful. The team members will meet at the departure airport at a designated time, typically much earlier than normally would be needed because someone is typically late, still allowing the team to catch the flight. Team members are expected to dress in their matching sweatsuits, which serve as advertisements for the club (as much as they also help the adults to keep track of them). The manager and/or coach carefully counts and checks off the players to avoid the nightmare scenario of leaving a kid behind. Then the team goes together to check in as a group. Teams typically try to avoid checking bags, especially ones including anything essential to playing in the games such as uniforms and cleats.

Teams that are geographically disadvantaged, such as those from Hawaii and Alaska, often fly long distances to participate in tournaments. Once the team arrives at its destination, rarely are team members and families able to go straight to the hotel. Rental cars or vans must be secured to transport them. Sometimes a few parents zip ahead to the rental agencies and secure the necessary transportation while the rest of the team waits at the airport. On other occasions, the entire team and accompanying adults pile onto the rent-a-car shuttle bus.

Subsequently, there are the inevitable lines associated with renting a car or van, however seasoned those leading this process are. Once rental cars or vans are secured, the team is finally on its way to the hotel, where the check-in process awaits. Team members already have their roommate assignments, keys are distributed, and the team is finally lodged.

What follows is typically a team meeting. The coach reminds the kids that they are at the tournament to play soccer, not to jump on the hotel beds or engage in similar antics. The level of compliance is more or less age appropriate. Some coaches encourage managers to organize activities and to allow swimming in the hotel pool, whereas other coaches forbid most ancillary activities because they view them as distractions from the purpose at hand, which is to win the tournament. This sort of attitude leaves bored kids stuck in their hotel rooms sleeping or on their smartphones. If a coach will allow ancillary activities such as an outing to a water park, families are expected to pay the costs. Wealthy families think nothing of footing the bill for such activities, but they can be quite a significant additional burden for families that already had to scrape just to pay the basic costs of sending their child to a travel tournament.

Feeding a youth-sports team as a group is another laborious aspect of tournament participation. If the team is to eat together at a restaurant, including coaches and accompanying parents, a reservation for about thirty must be secured. The team must be transported to the restaurant. At the restaurant, the ordering process is lengthy, but eventually the team is fed and then transported back to the hotel. As an alternative to a restaurant, experienced managers often reserve a meeting room at the hotel and have takeout brought in. Good managers are like officers directing the troops, but the monumental amount of time and effort expended is disproportionate to the amount of soccer minutes to be played.

For all the travel tournaments we have attended for our children's teams, not once has a team hotel been even remotely within walking distance of the playing fields. In some cases, the hotel was more than an hour's drive from the fields. Massive soccer complexes like 60 Acres outside of Seattle, in Redmond, Washington, with a total of 25 soccer fields, tend to be built away from businesses and hotels. These commutes back and forth to the fields are often longer than the games, contributing to the overall dead time.

Hopefully Raising the Championship Cup

While tournaments tend to be three-day events, they sometimes run four days. Many but far from all tournaments take place during the summer, but even the summer tournaments rest on certain assumptions. In order to get the players to the tournament and have them chaperoned, there must be enough parents who can take off a Friday and sometimes a Thursday or who have flexible jobs that allow them to work remotely. This assumption, combined with costs, shapes the socioeconomic makeup of the families who participate in the tournament circuit.

A typical team's schedule includes a group-round game on Friday and then two more group-round games on Saturday. In order to fit in all the games for all the age groups, which adds up to hundreds and hundreds, games are typically shorter than normal. For example, at the U-18 level, when a game typically lasts 90 minutes, games are often shortened to 60 minutes, making each minute of soccer played all the more precious—and expensive.

There is an array of formats to determine which teams advance to the knockout round. Some tournaments only guarantee three group games, with the requirement that a team win its group in order to advance into the playoffs. This means that as many as 75 percent of participating teams experience "three and done." The pressure to perform is intense, and the need to win each game is palpable. In other tournaments, the top two teams in a group of, say, four teams will go through, somewhat alleviating the pressure to win every game. (Few experts in youth sports, especially in reference to younger children, equate pressure to win as being compatible with healthy development, including development of players who go on to play at a high level.)

The pressure at these tournaments is on display even to the casual onlooker. There are of course good coaches. But there are also the coaches who yap endlessly at their players from first to last whistle. In fact, one of the defining features of tournaments is screaming coaches. Thoughtful observers conclude that some of the yapping is really a performance for the parents, to try to make it clear to the paying parents that the coach did all he could to "coach" the players and so if they lose it is the players' fault, not the coach's. Parents can turn viciously against coaches, so clearly some coaches try to preempt that with play-by-play scripting of the game. This is in spite of the fact that soccer requires that players develop creativity—the ability to make spur-of-the-moment decisions on the field rather than following play-by-play instructions.

The harm such yelling inflicts is multifaceted. Young players become so fearful of making a mistake that they do not try new things. Most adults do not like being yelled at, and neither do kids, so is there any wonder that many kids exit youth sports after experiencing coaches who are quick to criticize? But with all the money spent on getting to a tournament, is it surprising that there is pressure on the coach to at least advance to the knockout stage, to get the extra game or games, and preferably hoist a trophy, through whatever short-term means necessary? Tournaments accentuate the overall focus on winning even at the youngest ages, but an overwhelming focus on winning is not developmentally helpful at younger ages.

Tournaments also bring out the mathematician parents. It is not unusual to see parents in hotel lobbies and cafés hunched over their laptops studying how the tournament organizers have devised the point-scoring system that will determine which teams advance. With a typical group round involving only four teams and the potential for ties in soccer particularly common, there needs to be in place a variety of tiebreakers and also perhaps ways for teams to earn points in order to avoid tiebreakers. So at some tournaments a team gets six points for a victory, one point for earning a shutout in that same victory, and one point each for the first three goals scored, for a possible total of ten points.

Other tournaments use systems more similar to those in major international soccer tournaments, with three points for a victory, one point for a tie, and no points for a loss. Tiebreakers come down to head-to-head results, goal differential, total goals scored, and even lowest disciplinary points—the fewest number of yellow and red cards received by the team. Whatever system a tournament uses, once the first round of group-game results are in, the calculations begin for advancement to the next round.

Results are revisited once the second group-round games are completed. For example, after a tie against an evenly matched opponent in the first or second game, simply winning one's remaining match or matches may not be sufficient. It may be necessary to pulverize the weakest team in the group in order to win on goal differential. Such situations hardly seem conducive to development and lead to the strange culture of one set of players, parents, and coaches whose kids are getting drubbed having to endure the opposing set of players, parents, and coaches clearly going all out to run up the score. Coaches are not above screaming out demands for more goals in the waning minutes of such games to reach the number needed to advance to the knockout stage.

The culture of winning over development influences parental behavior. A majority of parents behave themselves most of the time, perhaps having to bite their tongues when their own child has been subjected to a dirty foul. Soccer is an intensely physical game, especially at the older ages, and nasty fouls can lead to devastating injuries. This makes it difficult for even the most restrained parents to sit idly by while their child is writhing on the ground after a nasty foul. Other parents seem to have adopted the attitude that the extraordinary amount of money they are shelling out for pay-to-play sports, especially for tournaments, includes free rein to abuse the referees endlessly. The amount of parental shouting at referees at tournaments would stun the uninitiated. Parents who watch the game in silence tend to find spots away from the shouters, who tend to group together as well.

At times, the shouters resemble a chorus, with each call or non-call not favoring one's team met with a cacophony of hisses and criticisms. One of the specificities of shouters at a soccer match is that they tend to be bloodthirsty to see players on the opposing team shown yellow cards for fouls. In fact, most players, even at the younger ages, brush off yellow cards as simply part of the game. But some parents see them differently.

Worldwide and in every sport, refereeing is a thankless job, but there is something primal about seeing frenzied parents at a tournament endlessly berating a referee for supposedly having wronged a U-11 team. Large tournaments often require hundreds of referees, so if there is a shortage, this means that the linespeople, often teenagers who need encouragement to continue their development into seasoned referees, are no less berated by parents who take out their anger at their team's performance on them.

The other common type of parent is the "advice giver." This parent wants to be a participant but can only do this by shouting out exhortations, instructions, and sports clichés. This parent is prone to screaming to the team such catch phrases as "wake up," "plenty of time left," "play the way you are capable of playing," "the more shots you take, the higher chance you have of scoring."

This is usually followed by a big no-no. In one such instance we witnessed at a boys soccer game, one of the players on the opposing team was contesting something with the referee in an appropriate manner, but then this father entered the discussion and told a player on the other team that he had seen exactly what had happened and that he was older and knew far more about soccer and that the referee's decision was correct. The frustrations piled up, and this father's son's team was not making headway on a deficit. So at this point the parent decided it was time to go solo, shouting to the son, "Sometimes you have to do it on your own!" The son ignored the unsolicited advice.

When the second half started, the parent, who was videotaping the game, shouted out: "Let's go guys, the camera is on." Apparently this was supposed to motivate the team, which seemed to be doing its best, to take it to a whole different level. The parent's contributions had a value of zero to negative because most kids hate when parents make spectacles of themselves at sporting events.

Parental distractions notwithstanding, one by one a team plays its three group-round games, keeping close track of how others in the group are doing. Frequently a team will have two games on a Saturday with no time for practice. At the older levels, intensely serious teams may arrive early to have one practice session on-site, but this is not the norm. One step down from the uber-serious teams, coaches might make time for a chalk talk about this or that strategy, but there is no on-field practice. Even if there were time to fit in a practice once the tournament has begun, there would likely be no fields available considering that tournaments often require every field in a radius of fifty miles or more from morning until nightfall. Highly sophisticated, monied clubs might have their older teams watch video footage of the games, trying to learn from that.

Here is what is missing. Most every umbrella governing sports organization that has taken the time to codify what is developmentally appropriate for young athletes prescribes some sort of formula according to which there should be a specified amount of practice time per game time—a ratio. Consider the "Player Development Model" provided on the United States Youth Soccer website, authored by Mike Smith.[19]According to this model, the recommended amount of practice time to game time increases at the older ages, becoming 2:1 by U-10, 3:1 by U-14, and at least 4:1 by U-19. Tournaments trample on this model, especially if a team attends tournaments on subsequent weekends.

According to the developmental model, which recommends a specific amount of practice time for each game played, a new skill is introduced and drilled during practices and then players are able to integrate it into games. This can be a slow process at the young ages. A few players try out the new skill in the first subsequent game, but the coaches must return to it in the next practice. Then in the subsequent game more players employ it.

But no practices take place during these tournaments. Kids replicate how they played in the previous game, for good or for bad. Additionally, the games take place in a pressurized setting that tends to discourage players from trying out new skills. No wonder that most thoughtful coaches have trouble taking tournaments seriously for their role in developing soccer, basketball, hockey, and other sports athletes, so estranged are tournaments from developmental models. The more tournaments a team takes part in, the more the coach ignores the recommended ratio of game to practice time.

Nonetheless, many coaches feel compelled to participate in tournaments because the pay-to-play industry, to a considerable extent, is predicated on these tournaments because they play a fundamental role in economically supporting many clubs. If one club tries to rein in the tournament mania, especially at the younger ages, parents may move their sons and daughters to another club that is taking its teams to faraway tournaments or to a club that features on its website the photo of the U-11 team hoisting the trophy at the Shangri-La Invitational.

We still have at our home a preposterously large trophy that a U-9 girls team, coached by our oldest daughter, who is now an adult, earned by winning a tournament. She remembers the near pandemonium as parents positioned themselves to photograph their daughters with the trophy, in spite of the fact that one of the 8-year-olds on the team had asked her coach, our daughter, completely seriously after the final game, "When is the championship game?" The 8-year old player was not even aware that her team had won the tournament. The oversized trophy remains at our home as a physical testament to what has penetrated youth sports for the purpose of stroking parental egos.

Depending on the prestige of the tournament, a big moneymaker for the club may be the club's own store selling memorabilia of the tournament including T-shirts, sweatshirts, and hats. The San Diego Surf Cup has branded itself as one of the most prestigious soccer tournaments in the United States. Walking into the Surf Cup's store, at the site of the fields, you can find simple T-shirts with Surf Cup markings selling for $40 because Surf Cup is something of a social signifier. The kid who walks around with a Surf Cup T-shirt sends a message to the pay-to-play soccer crowd: "I play on a team that was invited to Surf Cup." For parents, the message advertised by Surf Cup wear is broadly similar: "Our child is on the high-level tournament circuit." But don't blame Surf Cup. It is simply playing by the rules of the market.

For many parents, tournaments are pleasant social scenes. Team outings in between games are a chance for the moms and dads to catch up and compare notes on everything from which coaches in the club are the best to whether they should jump to another club that goes to even more tournaments to how to attract the attention of college coaches. During the day and especially at nighttime, only a small contingent of chaperones are needed to mind the kids, so parents can steal away for a quiet dinner out together as a twosome or with another couple.

It is common that players are required to be in their rooms by 9 p.m., with lights out by 10. For some parents this is a chance to head to the bar, where, with a little luck, they might encounter one of the coaches and be able to buy him or her a drink, ingratiating themselves with the coach and hopefully sneaking in a mention that their son or daughter really prefers playing central midfield to outside midfield. Many coaches avoid these situations, keeping secret where they are going for dinner and drinks with other coaches from the clubs at the tournament, some of whom are old friends. But some coaches struggle mightily with maintaining proper boundaries with parents, especially since blurring these boundaries can result in tangible benefits, such as offers to use a family's vacation home for a weekend.

The next day, the group round is over. Many teams have been eliminated, usually at least half or more, although there are tournaments that send more than half of the participating teams on to the knockout stage or provide additional consolation matches.

Consider the contrast between these tournaments and the practices of some countries, notably France, that do an extraordinary job of developing soccer players. There is no score kept in youth-soccer matches in France until the mid-teen years.[20] In contrast, the American tournament system makes it explicit who failed and who succeeded in a high-pressure environment. Teams advancing to the knockout round in some cases did whatever was necessary to earn the requisite points against the team that had mistakenly entered the tournament simply for fun.

There is a frenzied competition among various entities to stage showcase tournaments, saturating the market, reducing the chance that college coaches can be in more than one place at any one time. For a few decades, the United States Youth Soccer Regionals enjoyed considerable cachet, but they have lost some of their luster as more and more MLS teams have developed youth academies and additional, parallel leagues have emerged that siphon away teams from participating in Regionals. Up until 2000 or so, United States Youth Soccer managed basically all organized youth soccer in the United States, but this is no longer the case. It has many competitors, U.S. Club Soccer for example, to which the United States Soccer Federation extended membership. What this has created, in practice, is a tremendous diffusion of players.

Another factor beyond thinned player ranks that further undermined the validity of the 2021 United States Youth Soccer Far West Regionals was a disturbingly large number of game results being defined by preposterous goal differentials. Does it really make sense to make State Cup champions from sparsely populated states kick off against champions from heavily populated states? With rare exceptions, the results are foretold.

In the U-18 age group, when as a rule blowouts should be rare, in a group-round game a team from Las Vegas, Nevada, beat the team from Montana 11–1, a veritable drubbing in soccer at that age. In the world of club soccer, teams from large metropolitan areas have a much larger, sometimes vastly larger, pool of youth players from which to draw, so there is no point matching these club teams up against teams from largely rural states. What is especially discouraging about these sorts of happenings at Regionals is that these are tournaments are administered by United States Youth Soccer, whose officials surely know better.

At tournaments, one and only one champion will be crowned. So, in order to win tournaments at young ages, all the time-tested rules for how to develop youth athletes from the long-term perspective go out the door. There are endless examples of how the tournament format encourages behavior that is not conducive to development. At higher levels of soccer, there are ways of wasting time in the latter stages of a game in order to shorten a game, thus securing a win or a tie. It is not an attractive part of the game, but when the stakes are high coaches make strategic subs not just to replace fatigued players but in order to disrupt the rhythm of the game, though at the higher levels the rules tend to limit the number of substitutions that can be made.

Incoming subs usually prolong the delay before free kicks and throw-ins are executed. Players can dribble the ball to the corner rather than attack their opponent's goal. This requires defenders to desperately try to regain possession in a situation that more often than not has them kicking the ball out of bounds or committing a foul. This results in yet another slow-motion throw-in, corner kick, or free kick, often used to take the ball to the corner yet again for more time wasting. All of this is part of the game at the higher levels, but should it be part of the game at the youth level?

Although there has been some progress in this area, youth coaches are typically less restricted in the number of substitutions they can make, resulting in the possibility of fully destroying the rhythm of a game, to the disadvantage of the team that is trying to equalize the score. Is it developmentally helpful for coaches to shout out to their players to take their time on free kicks and order players to take the ball to the corner and try to waste time? Even young players have seen professional players do this, but there is something chilling about hearing a U-11 coach trying to secure a victory by screaming at a 10-year-old to take the ball to the corner.

These sorts of tactics are easily learned at a later stage. It is not as though players need to be groomed from a young age so that the rare player who ends up playing at a high level knows what to do in these situations. At the younger ages it would be better if coaches specifically advised players against using such tricks. After all, shortening the amount of time through deliberate time-wasting methods when players have the opportunity to actually touch the ball and compete in the game helps players on neither side further develop their skills.

But there must be a tournament champion here in the United States, which in the case of soccer even includes concluding matches at the youngest levels with penalty kicks. Penalty kicks are a measure that governing associations at the highest level of soccer came up with in order to decide which team advances in major tournaments when matches remain tied after overtime. They are a necessary evil for higher levels of soccer competition, but must this ritual that often leaves one kid in tears for having missed a deciding penalty kick be extended down to the youngest age groups? The answer in the tournament circuit is yes. There must be a champion, and there must be photographic evidence of the championship team.

The cost analysis of just how much a family pays for each minute of tournament soccer should not be misunderstood as an endorsement of lengthening the games—far from it. Another fundamental problem with tournaments is the compressed nature of the game schedule. The winning team and runner-up will typically end up playing five games in about 48 hours, an intense schedule even with shortened games that will, over time, take its toll on young bodies in the form of overuse injuries. It is no medical secret that fatigued muscles are especially prone to injury. Jamming as much game time into the short timeframe that tournaments must follow is contrary to long-term development from the additional perspective of the needless injuries that result. The tournaments are only part of an overall culture of overuse, but they are an especially intense form of that culture.

There have been some efforts at reform in this area, with the MLS Next League inserting a day of rest in tournament schedules. So four days are required to fit in three games. But MLS Next is the exception to the rule. Rest days are costly, at least in the short term, for all involved, so best to fit as many games into as short a period as possible. The consequences of this, such as the costs of repairing blown-out knees, for example, are never factored in.

With the champion crowned and the requisite photo of the happy players holding up the trophy snapped, members of both teams typically dash for the rental vehicles to get to the airport to catch flights. But most of the teams who were eliminated on Saturday will also take Sunday-evening flights home because it is impossible to predict who will advance to the final. Knocked out of the tournament, these teams spend an extra day often doing nothing more than killing time.

For some tournaments, it is even worse. At the Regional and National tournaments sponsored by United States Youth Soccer, there are four days between the day when a team could be knocked out and when the championship match is played. This means that teams that travel by plane and find themselves out of the tournament at the conclusion of games on Wednesday may still have to wait around until Sunday evening to catch their flights. In order to avoid this scenario, many teams wisely choose monumental drives that at least provide flexibility. But for the teams from afar that cannot rearrange flight schedules, what to do with these extra days? It is a chance to see a new place, to perhaps visit an amusement park or a water park, or simply play miniature golf, but this comes at extra expense. Older teams might visit a few colleges. But regardless of what additional activities might be scheduled, it is a lot of additional time and money.

Soccer teams returning from tournaments exhibit a noticeable number of banged-up and bruised players. Many are icing their bodies. Some have new injuries that require crutches. Occasionally players must be transported through the airport by wheelchair. Parents of the badly injured are already scheduling visits to doctors as well as appointments with physical therapists in their hometowns. If this were a professional team returning with wounded bodies from one of its matches, observers would attribute it to unavoidable job-related hazards that are offset by high salaries.

What term best describes the situation in reference to youth teams? Terms such as "neglect" or even "abuse" come to mind, but what is obvious is how divorced the tournament circuit is from thought-ful development of youth athletes. The number of youth players who are felled by injuries has reached epidemic proportions, and spending a year rehabilitating from a devastating ACL injury—now common among teenage soccer players, especially girls—is hardly conducive to development. The tournament circuit is not solely responsible for the overuse-injury epidemic, but it is a significant contributing fac-tor. The tournament circuit sucks up immense monetary and time resources from families while giving little back in terms of develop-ment. Nowhere else, including in other wealthy countries, is it being emulated as a means to develop young athletes. Rather, it is the object of disdain and scorn worldwide among those who know better how to develop athletes.

Chapter 4

A Road Map for Navigating Pay-to-Play Sports

*[Today's youth sports] emphasize performance over partici-
pation well before kids' bodies, minds, and interests mature.
And we tend to value the child who can help win games or
whose families can afford the rising fees. The risks for that
child are overuse injuries, concussion, and burnout.*[21]

"Prestige" word origin: derived from Latin **praestigium** *for
"delusion" or "illusion." Original use of the word prestige
meaning "trick" from the French word for "deceit."*[22]

Who Is Driving the Train and Who Is Making the Decisions?

After hours of discussions with our three children, their peers' parents,
and family members who went down this path with our nieces and
nephews before we did, we have learned a lot about parenting through
the Youth Sports Industry. These friends' and families' athletes have
had similar experiences but also notable differences punctuating how
positive or negative their youth-sports years were. Our single most
important observation navigating this industry and its myriad webs
was, How much does a child love to play? For example, once a child
turns 16, working at a part-time job in order to help defray the costs
of pay-to-play can be a pretty fair indicator of whether the child loves
the game.

Or do the parents take more responsibility for their child's sporting performance than the child does? Do they love their child playing the sport more than the child loves playing the sport? And if the child loves to play the sport, is he or she allowed to decide when the playing days are over? At the end of every sports season, difficult to define now in year-round sports, or at the very least before parents sign the next year's financial-commitment contract, have they asked their child if he or she wants to play again the following year? And are they honestly prepared to let their child walk away without worried lectures about dedication and commitment and long-term impact on college-admissions chances through success in extracurriculars, and on and on, no matter the age or talent level, if the child says no?

If parents say it is up to their child but act like it is not, then the child is very likely not driving the train. If they will not let the child walk away from the sport, then the child is not driving the train. And they should be on the lookout for overinvolved coaches and clubs who are attempting to sell the dream to their child—and to you—for their own financial, emotional, prestige, or victory gains. Parents, do not permit them to take over decisions that are not theirs to make for your child.

Who is driving the college-athletics recruiting process within a high school–aged club-sports program? Is it the club recruitment specialist, the coach, the parent, or the child? Who is sending out monthly or weekly reminders about the recruiting process, and why are they sending them? Athletic-recruiting consultants' roles can closely resemble the role of a private-college admissions coach. But, by definition, is this a process that requires the participation of all youth athletes? The more-successful placements at prestigious colleges are front and center on a sports club's website, the better for their bottom line but not necessarily the happiness of the players.

What about those times when a child no longer wants to be playing the game after high-school years but is still prodded and poked with prestigious dream enticements to get recruited? Wise parents understand that their child should be driving the train of how much importance this sport plays in his or her life. If the child wants help, he or she should be encouraged to ask from where and from whom help is needed to accomplish sports goals. And if the child does not want the help, parents should be quiet and respect their child's right to make this call. This is an enormous sea change in attitude and behavior adjustment for many parents who have spent years hovering, helicoptering, and setting the table for success on a daily basis for their child, whether the child wants to eat at that particular success table or not.

If a child wants to accomplish the goal of gaining admission and playing a sport in college, that is a train the child absolutely should drive. Just because the child could play a sport at some college, does that by definition mean that he or she should? Is not the person who will be spending those college years dedicating countless hours a week to the sport, enduring injuries, navigating coaches' demands, and responding or failing to meet the relentless time-management challenges involved with being a scholar-athlete the one who should be deciding whether or not to do this? The child must decide how much importance this sport still plays, and may play, for at least the next four years.

For all but the 10 percent—or typically fewer, depending on the sport[23]—of college athletes who go on to play at a professional or semi-professional level, that means four more years of playing that sport. And for some, they are a less than ideal four more years of playing in college than had been hyped to be the holy grail worth sacrificing anything and everything in their youth. If a child decides not to play a college sport, this is not a life success–ending path to doom. Maybe the player would finally have the time and opportunity to develop other interests and other ways to contribute to the college community, personal growth, and enjoyment of the college experience. Wouldn't it be refreshing to see club-sports websites highlight the character- and citizenship-related life accomplishments of their athlete alumni first, and second, if at all, what level of sport they did or did not choose to pursue after their club-sports experience.

In late middle-school or early high-school years, assuming parents have their children decide each year if they still want to play, and they are still playing, these children need to be given realistic expectations from both their parents and the coaches about the chances of obtaining a college-sports-team position, including the work that will be required of them and nobody else. Just ask any college coach what he or she thinks about the desirability of a potential recruit whose communications have all been prepared, sold, and packaged by someone other than the athlete.

Even if there are always more and more "advantages" that parents can buy, sometimes they are in fact making things worse for their child by buying them. What parents want is not always what their child wants, and what their child wants the child should be able to earn. At the very least, in what used to be one of the last frontiers of merit, a spot on a college-sports team should be earned by the child's hard work and abilities.

Why is a high school–age club team so invested in which colleges and how many of its former athletes went on to play at a college level? Are many clubs more excited about college-placement advising than coaching and developing players in their sport and teaching life lessons? Perhaps the answer is good-hearted club-team businesspeople with their eyes on a long-term business model: Who will be our next poster child that will capture the prestige-seeking parents for the next ten years?

Do not discount the impact of overinvolved parents and coaches driving a train that is unquestionably the child's to drive. Children need mentoring along the way, from the very first steps in the yard with a ball, to trust their bodies, trust their emotions, work hard, and love the game until they cannot or do not want to play it anymore. And if they are working with or living with adults in the sport who will not honor their bodies, emotions, work, and love of the game, it is time for some careful and immediate attention to the situation.

We have been chided, scolded, and derided along the way by fellow parents who insist on a singular focus on one parenting maxim: The adult knows what is best for the child and must make the decisions. Why have we two as parents allowed our children at such young ages to make their own decisions in youth sports, which appeared so contrary to the norms of the athletic-prestige chasers? We must be too permissive, or we must just not be in the know like the "true and dedicated, all-in" sports-parent elite, mused our fellow parents.

We and our son were left out along the way from a group of parents who gathered an exclusive bundle of players on the team to give them special, extra, and costly training on the side so they could "stay ahead of the Joneses." It stunned us, but in hindsight they likely knew before we did that we would not sing the parent-group tune to help one another feel good about parental overinvolvement. And several of these needlessly overtrained kids' interests in soccer lasted no longer than middle school.

We have done our honest best along this lifelong-learning parenting journey to trust our children in what they aspire to in their lives, not ours, and to allow this trust to foster our lifelong relationships with them. And we have made our fair share of mistakes along the way. But wise parents know that they will more likely than not make many wrong decisions along the way and are willing to eat humble pie to correct those mistakes as soon as possible. We tried to balance the competing truths of the parent-knows-best model with the child-knows-best paradigm at every step of our parenting journey, knowing that these decisions are rarely either-or situations, especially when it comes to youth sports.

We believe in leaving the decisions that should truly be the child's to decide to the child, regardless of age. We lent our guidance and thoughts and protection along the way, but ultimately the decision was our daughters' or son's. We also believe in making the decisions that are ours as parents to decide. As an example covering both parties: A child decides if he or she wants to play; the parents decide if they want their child to play (perhaps for safety reasons) or can even pay for it. When these two decisions get mixed up, as in the parents who try to make the child play, and the child who tries to make the parents pay, this is where things can go terribly wrong.

Is the child trusted by the parents when he says, I love this sport but I also want to have time to go fishing on the weekends? Is the child trusted when she says, I love this sport but I also want to have time with my close friends who do not play my sport? Is the child trusted by the coach when he says I really like it and I want to play this sport but for fun in high school and not to pursue college-level recruiting, no matter how talented the club coach insists he is? Is the child trusted by the parent when she says, I am tired of this sport and I want to try a new sport that looks more fun, no matter how talented others judge her to be at the sport she is currently playing?

Is the child trusted when he says, my arm hurts and I want to stop, no matter how much the team needs his talented arm? Is the child trusted when she says this is a terrible team culture and I want out? Is the child trusted when he says I am tired of all this practicing, even if all this practicing is exactly what the coach is recommending and the coach is telling the parents how much potential the child has? Is the child trusted when she says this coach is a mean jerk who demands that kids who are off task sit in a corner with a dunce cap on and I don't want to play for that coach anymore?

Over the years we learned that our three kids, from their youngest ages, were spot-on judges of which coaches were great, good, pretty good, mediocre, bad, or horrific. Their ability to articulate exactly what made a coach good or bad developed as they grew older, but they knew good from bad from their earliest years in organized sports. Cumulatively, our kids had at least one coach fitting into each of the above categories, with a disconcerting number of the pay-to-play, paid professionals, being in the pretty good to mediocre category.

Trust does not mean that the entire decision is left completely up to the child but that parents take the feedback from their child extremely seriously with careful, thoughtful discussions to follow. Trust means the parents will carefully weigh what the coaches say against what the child says and never assume that if the adult coach is recommending something by definition it must always be what is right for the child. In many cases it is what is right for the coach for that club's success. Trust does not necessarily mean that the child gets to immediately stop the commitment to the team until the end of the season, but in some cases it might.

If there is no situation in the parents' mind that would allow a young athlete to pause on a commitment to improve in the area of sports and chances for future success and prestige, the child is in danger and is definitely not driving the train. But for many parents, there might be only one exception, such as a serious physical injury. But what about all the indicators that the child is drowning in emotional turmoil or that the body is breaking down from overuse as a result of participating in the misguided model of the Youth Sports Industry? Would these be reasons the child is allowed to walk away from the "promise of success"? A sport is supposed to be fun for a kid, even when hard work and discipline are essential to playing the game well.

In many families, the parents consider themselves the foremost authorities on, and decision-makers for, their child, at least until the child is considered a self-supporting adult. But what if the parental authorities do not know, or will not allow themselves to know, to give a not-so-extreme example anymore, that there is a sexually abusive coach involved with their child's team? What if parents deny all the warning signs and their child's distress about a severe physical injury, all in hopes of securing the highest level of athletic prestige? And all for what? It is hard or impossible for an athlete to win the Olympic gold or to "go pro" when they have died by suicide or had their career ended by physical injuries, all because they were not allowed to walk away by the adults who insisted that they knew better how to develop and protect those children's glorious futures.

A Lifestyle Choice: The Real Costs in Time and Money

What are the real costs in time and money for participation in the current Youth Sports Industry from ages 5 on up to 18? If it were only the costs to those parents who freely choose to allow their children to play, and for them to spend their personal time and money on a youth-sports club program, what would the big deal be? The real national cost of this model is that far too many children have no opportunity to play in their own neighborhoods anymore. No fields, no low-cost programs, no gyms, no recreational centers, no coaches, no access. And for those parents who can afford it, the costs to many of these children can be a lost childhood. The price paid by participating youth is sometimes a childhood largely lost to injuries, anxiety, depression, and burnout.

Here is what our time commitment in the years we spent in the Youth Sports Industry looked like. The older two of of our three children were lucky to have a generous grandmother; by the time our son began pay-to-play, grandmotherly subsidies were no longer required for us to support this endeavor. All played multiple sports from about the age of 5. With two drivers in the household, we sometimes had three kids needing to go to different fields at the same time before they started getting their licenses. And even with extra family drivers, if it was three kids on three different fields, that required at least three cars or a very complex carpool schedule. All played for some amount of time on multiple club-sports teams, often with overlapping seasons. All played their main sport in high school. The hours and the money spent detailed here are conservative.

Time for one child:
- Practices per week: 2–3, with drive time 90–120 minutes per practice
- Practices per week at high-school age: If playing for the high-school team (for a different sport) and a club-sports team, potentially totaling 16 hours per week
- Games per weekend: 2; 4–5 for tournament play
- Drive time: Up to 7 hours round-trip for certain games in Oregon or Washington
- Tournaments at high school-age per year: 12, 4–5 by plane

Costs for one child annually for U-14 and above:
- Club fees: $1,500–$2,000
- Tournament fees: $600

- Airfare for tournaments: $2,000
- Airfare and registration for ID camps: $4,000–$5,000
- Hotels: $1,500
- Tryout fees: $50
- Uniforms: $350
- Equipment: $300
- Indoor/Futsal: $200

Total annual cost for one child:
- $6,500–$7,000, with $4,000–$5,000 for ID camps and more for any special clinics

Good Clubs, Good Coaches, Good Data

Parents should demand to know more. The parental bill payers and consumers of the Youth Sports Industry are the linchpins to its survival. We all vote with our wallets, and despite the unrelenting arms-race pressure of "the Joneses are paying for this so we need to," substantial word-of-mouth and social-media power in the parental community can insist upon programs with the long-term health and interests of our youth in mind.

Unfortunately, to date the only organized parental movement we have observed is prestige-driven parents who run complex political campaigns within the parent-team communities to organize families to leave good, thoughtful coaches and teams for last season's more successful team and club. This departure campaign is most often driven by whether or not little Susie got enough minutes of playing time at her favorite position in the most recent State Cup game and whether the "amazing" team actually failed to live up to expectations by losing the State Cup that spring. Many parents spend an inordinate amount of time researching the prestige, win-loss performance records, and college-placement successes of the clubs we gladly allow to attach a syphon to our bank accounts. But it is what we parents do not routinely ask for or research about sports clubs that needs to change.

Look on your club's website or speak with your club's director about the team's philosophies on the long-term-development model versus the skills-and-excellence model of youth sports.[24] Observe carefully to confirm that the practice of these philosophies matches the website mission statements and the annual beginning-of-the-season speech rhetoric. One useful red flag is how coaches are training and employing the "early developers." Are they using them at young ages to win, to the detriment of long-term development not only on the part of the early developer but also all the other players?

If they work primarily within the skills-and-excellence model, how do they address the risks associated with early specialization and year-round participation in a single sport? What are the training requirements of the coaches at every level of youth development? What training do the coaches receive in understanding child emotional and physical development as it relates to what is being asked of the players at specific ages? What first-aid training is required of the coaches? What is the club's policy on reporting suspected child abuse or maltreatment by coaches or parents?

What is the retention rate of players at each of the age groups? Is the club truly focused on developing the players it already has or on recruiting new players from where the grass is greener. We remember vividly our son's experience playing up for a U-11 team at one of the local clubs and how the coach (whose English accent gave him an air of authority) waxed eloquently about development. Meanwhile, this coach blatantly subcontracted to parents on the team the duty of recruiting the better players from the club's opponents. It was a well-organized poaching exercise. The parents made targeted invitations to birthday parties and the like, and the operation proved immensely successful.

But then there was a remarkable moment after tryouts at the first meeting of the next season between the parents and the coach. One parent, who had probably been a late developer physically, asked precisely how poaching multiple players from opposing teams in the short term aligned with the focus on development in the long term.

Rather than answering what might have been the single most coura-geous question we ever heard a parent ask in one of these meetings, the coach, who was clearly flustered at being called to task, went on a bizarre ramble about how he was a "type-A personality" and it was best not to push him too hard.

Additional questions parents need answers to: What is the injury rate of the players across the age spans of the club? Does the club keep the injury-rate data from year to year, and what is it doing to address any trends? Of the players and families who leave the club mid-year or after several years, does the club do exit interviews or anonymous surveys to assess the primary reason for leaving? Is the club willing to make gen-eral findings accessible to parents who are interested in joining the club?

Parents who care about their child's physical and emotional health more than their child's college-scholarship prospects as the greatest return on investment that youth sports might bring them would insist that clubs answer these questions. If we demand that clubs be cogni-zant of the known problems associated with the Youth Sports Industry and show thoughtful plans of how they are attempting to correct vari-ous problems, including those that present immediate risks to our chil-dren, we may begin to turn this ship around.

Finally, however good a club is overall, much comes down to the coach. Take into account whether the individual is new to coaching as it does no good to destroy the trajectory of a promising young coach who, admittedly, has some growing to do. Your child cannot have the best coach in the club every year. But higher standards should be expected of long-term coaches. For example, does the coach, with-out fail, begin and end on time a well-organized and fun practice that is developing young athletes? Does the coach clearly communicate expectations and policies? Does the coach follow through consistently on these expectations and policies?

Kids are legendarily capable of sniffing out when coaches, or any figures of authority for that matter, do not apply expectations and policies consistently (e.g., are certain players somehow excused from following policies because the coach needs a win this weekend?) and correspondingly lose respect for the coach. Does the coach know enough about the game to reinforce immediately and positively when a player is demonstrating command of a new skill or tactic? What is the ratio of positive reinforcement to criticism?

If your child, even at a young age, expresses a negative opinion about a coach, neither brush it off nor take it too seriously before discussing it. What is it that your child does not like about the coach? If your child is upset that the coach had Johnnie play goalie in last weekend's game rather than your child, then the complaint has no broader validity, and make that clear to your child. But observations by kids about coaches more often than not do have validity, along the following lines: "I already practice juggling the ball at home so I don't see why we all had to juggle for the first 45 minutes of practice while the coach texted on his phone." Even if the coach had not been on the phone, there is really no justification for 45 minutes of a practice being devoted to something that can just as easily be practiced on one's own. This is not good coaching; it is babysitting.

Directors of clubs will pay almost no attention to parental complaints about playing time or even wins and losses in reference to one of their coaches, so parents might want to save their breaths in this area, which presently constitutes the majority of parental complaints. But club directors will sit up if a reasoned argument can be made that a coach should be provided remedial counseling or even be fired because he or she arrived late to multiple practices and games, ran disorganized practices, did not seem to have much energy left over to reinforce with excited, positive feedback when a player had demonstrated improvement in practice, and generally seemed to be phoning in his or her considerable responsibilities as coach. Of course there are instances of downright abuse that should be reported immediately. But should we pay for long-term mediocrity? If someone has been coaching for years and is still in the mediocre-to-bad category, the situation should not be tolerated.

This is tricky territory because many parents complain relentlessly already, so much so that the number-one grievance of coaches is having to deal with entitled parents. But parents should not be silent. Rather, they should redirect their eyes and feedback to different areas, such as supplementing their common sense about what makes a good coach by reading about great coaches to develop clear standards in their minds (making sure that these standards are applied in an age-appropriate way). Unsurprisingly, there is much overlap between what makes for a great coach and what makes for a great teacher or a great supervisor or a great military officer. It is not too much to ask to hold a coach to certain standards.

Who Will Be Your Family's and Your Child's Best Advocate?

Financial Health: At first glance, this would seem to be the easiest area in which to provide guidance to parents. What is good for the financial health of the family is good for the financial health of the child and their overall relational health. If a family cannot afford to have a child participate in the Youth Sports Industry, then it should not be done. It can only be hoped that the current grossly inaccessible Youth Sports Industry that marches on despite cries for change for decades will crash and burn and that legislatures will make desperately needed funding changes to make organized sports accessible to children from families of all income levels. But until that time the Youth Sports Industry remains a money-devouring creature that cleverly manipulates parents' fears about lost opportunity.

The spider cleverly weaves a web of fact omission to remove any doubt whatsoever parents may have about the need to pay every penny of the staggering costs of playing. Is it really worth going into debt to attempt to ensure that your child has the chance to play at a college level? Is it worth delaying savings and retirement investments[25]-that will make it very likely the family cannot afford retirement, thus burdening the child with multiple future financial burdens? Even if there is a rare partial or full athletic scholarship in the picture, the tuition-cost savings in most cases might not even come close to exceeding the amount parents have paid for roughly thirteen years to the Youth Sports Industry.

How might a family save some money if it decides to have a child participate? How many extra clinics are highly encouraged or facilitated by a club? If in the winter season the coach is strongly recommending that the 10-year old players participate in, for example, speed and agility clinics at extra cost, might parents ask if there is actually a problem with their child's speed and agility? Or is the unspoken assumption that more is always better.

If the child might also be working on speed and agility in the off-season (or the "relatively off-season" for year-round sports) in a different sport or activity, even with cross-training benefits, might that be a good reason to pass on the extra clinic? This decision may be considered by coaches and other parents to be sacrilege, risky, not politically savvy, not "all-in," too independent, and yet it is smart, especially financially smart, for many families. But how many parents dare say no to the coach who holds the magic strings of playing time and can grant their child the right to "dance" or to sit out for the shame of nondedication to the whole program?

Is it really better for the financial, social, and emotional health of the family and the player to only take "vacations" for team tournaments since there is no time or cash left for perhaps 98 percent of families to have a vacation anywhere else? And if the exhausted and overstretched working parents have somehow found the time to identify where the relentless sports-game calendar appears to have one or two consecutive free weekends in a summer, beware of the last minute "by the way, our team is traveling to Europe this summer" email from the coach. Oh, and yes, the parents will be in charge of the fund-raising and will of course pay for all of the coaches' travel expenses.

Yes, parents can say they are not available to participate in a trip and are not available to help with hours of fund-raising events. And yes, the coach may find someone else to come up from a younger age group or over from another team as a visiting player who will gladly pay the costs of the trip and take your child's spot. And yet, usually, the club and team will be ready for you to pay for your player's next trip and next season, even when you dared to decline. Clubs and coaches who understand boundaries will have reasonable conversations with families about these matters and can most often work out mutually agreeable compromises. So, dare to try.

Team Health: There are examples of coaches and club directors who know how to empower families to feel that they can have a strong say in how much money they can or want to invest in their child's travel for sports. One of the finest examples we encountered was the coach of a U-12 boys-club soccer team who correctly recognized early in the fall season that he had a strong, talented team that appeared to be dominant in the state of Oregon at that point in time. He was planning the season ahead and invited the parents to a team meeting, where we were asked to vote on three different local-driving or air-travel options. The experienced, secure, and widely successful coach calmly told the families he was not there to insist that they spend their money traveling and that he could find plenty of ways to develop this team locally if the families did not clearly and strongly approve the costly travel options. The majority parental vote was not to travel. The coach did not look for other players to step on to the team to let the team travel, we did not travel by plane, and this was zero impediment to the development of these young athletes.

That year was a great team experience. The team did not "get worse" or lose a few games locally by the end of the season because they dared not to fly off to "better competition." On the contrary, they were a very successful team that made it to the Oregon State Cup final, had a fine performance but lost in PKs—considered a coin flip by those who know soccer. Yet ask a pay-to-play coach why a team must travel and see how many times you will hear the travel myth: Teams must travel to get better. Ask a typical pay-to-play coach how precisely participation in a tournament made the team better and also how it made each individual player better. But some myths are so accepted as truth that no one takes the time to question them.

Our exceptional coach stuck with his plans for that team and refused to pull in other "recruits" mid-season to make an already strong team into a steamrolling behemoth. How refreshing to see this coach dedicated to developing these players on this team in this local area instead of chasing the "win now at all cost and must travel" Youth Sports Industry norm. This coach occasionally explained why he did not intervene at times that less-experienced coaches might have felt the pressure to do so in the name of short-term wins: "Some of the players on the team dribble too much, but they are still very young. I am not going to crush their creativity before it has even blossomed. Expectations will change as they grow older."

For many coaches, identifying new and promising talent can be one of the most exciting parts of coaching. But overdedication of priorities, time, and resources to the "clear future stars" is a short-sighted, negligent, and often misguided strategy. The future "star" at age 12 very often does not look at all like a star any more at 18, and all coaches with even a small amount of experience can tell you that. We do not know if this wonderful coach was being entirely frank when he claimed that as a basic rule he did not have the slightest idea which 11-year-olds might develop into talented older players; did he not have some inkling in a few cases over his long coaching career during which he had nurtured several professional players? But this viewpoint is actually far closer to reality than coaches who claim pre-science. Nonetheless, some coaches cannot help but boldly and exclusively pursue the development of quite young athletes who have what they interpret to be the stuff of higher-level promising talent. But how often does this pan out, even after a considerable amount of money has been remitted by a family to a club?

If coaches are not assigned to an Olympic-team coaching position, and even if they are, they have a responsibility to develop every athlete on their team. They have a responsibility to believe in developing the personal best in all of their players and to create a team culture in which all players' roles and contributions are valued no more than the others, regardless of the level of talent and competition for that team.

To paraphrase the legendary coach Clive Charles, who arguably did more to develop soccer in the Greater Portland area than any other coach, if the 24th player in terms of talent on a roster of 24 players does not think that he or she is as important as all the other players, then the coach is not doing his or her job. If the current popular American skills and excellence model instead had a nationally organized youth-athlete-development system more closely resembling that of the long-term Athletic Development Model used in Canada, or the American Development Model adopted by USA Hockey in 2009,[26] many of the systemic issues that allow for neglecting the health and opportunity for millions of our youth would be resolved.

Adult-Driven Pressure to Stay and Play: The year-round pay-to-play system admittedly puts high-school coaches, athletes, and their families in quandaries that were far less common a generation ago. Previously it was considered normal for a high-school coach to expect that participants in a sport devote themselves to that sport almost exclusively in season, with consequences in terms of playing time if they did not. But the pay-to-play system raises new problems. Consider the following example. A kid has a commitment to his pay-to-play soccer club team, but he would love to play on the high-school basketball team in season as well. Is there a way for coaches, athletes, and families to navigate reasonable expectations in this situation? Yes, but it is new and tricky territory.

Any hope of navigating this situation successfully will likely require fitting two additional meetings into the schedules of various parties, one with the athlete and high-school coach (it is sometimes best that the parents be present for this meeting too, depending on many factors) and another with the athlete and club coach (ditto on the parents being present). The combination of high-school coaches who, not without justification, would like to see in-season commitment, and club coaches who demand year-round commitment, makes it increasingly difficult for kids who want to be multisport high-school athletes to do so.

What if coaches and players alike could discuss collaboratively how to handle competing conflicts as they now exist for the multisport athlete or for the athlete who is also talented at another extracurricular pursuit? What if coaches could talk to each other at the beginning of the season about the conflicts that the athlete presents and decide among themselves if compromises can be reached? In order to protect youth athletes from these pressures, some states have gone as far as requiring a contract be signed that an athlete cannot play on both a club team and a high-school team at the same time.

What if the other athletes on the team could be consulted by the coach to see if they felt that the fact the athlete who missed due to another sports-related conflict would harm the team "irreparably"? What if the coach could say that of course it is okay to miss practice once in a while as long as it was manageable for the team? What if every level of player on the team was as important as the next and they were all trained to be prepared for when the team needed them to step up and step in?

Perhaps the team might win fewer games, or perhaps the team might win more. Perhaps the team would have players out on the field or the court who knew they were there fully of their own choosing and not in fear of losing the "love and approval" of the coach and they would play with the heart and commitment of something freely chosen and freely let go of, in the true spirit of the definition of play. When they actually become professionals, maybe then their coaches and their paid contracts call those shots, but not at the high-school level. What if the majority of high-school and college athletes could again be seen as those who "play" sports instead of "work" sports for the adults who run them?

Some of the less-appealing aspects of the Youth Sports Industry have unsurprisingly migrated into the high-school setting, even as some high-school administrators try to preserve all that is good about high-school sports. Parents of a certain generation cannot even fathom the possibility that in our high-school sports years there might have been a coach who called a parent-team meeting to discuss the participation expectations and commitment of the players including beyond the time frame of the season itself.

These parents cannot imagine in their wildest dreams that a high-school coach would be expecting and relentlessly encouraging youth athletes to play more of that sport in the form of a pay-to-play club sport during the high-school off-season to demonstrate their dedication and commitment to the following year's high-school team. In our high-school years, kids tried out for the team at the start of the season and either made it or did not. We played on the team and enjoyed it, to return for another season, or tried something new the next year. Of course there were young athletes who did practice that sport in the off-season, but it was not an expectation. And yet, forty years after our high-school sports years, there are high-school coaches who view participation in the Youth Sports Industry as a means to add additional trophies won by their high-school teams to the cases on display in the school corridor.

Some high-school coaches tell young athletes that they have not trained enough year-round to prepare them for their next high-school season. Parents of naturally gifted athletic children must be especially on guard to help guide their children through the maze of conflicting expectations because it can be the case that the coach of nearly every high-school sport would like to convince a child to make that sport the singular focus, or in any case a predominant focus, including the joining of a pay-to-play club. Players are cajoled into costly private training sessions, badgered to join the newest local club team, sent required off-season drills and workouts, and, during the pandemic, required to join Zoom workouts to keep up their skills, and so on. They must stay in touch with the team and continually commit.

And if they do not? It is seen as the child's deficiency instead of a systemic-level conflict of interest. If certain high-school athletes do not want to play all year-round, their loyalty is questioned and their dollars are not supporting the club team whose coaches often have a dual conflict of being both a high-school coach and a club coach or club director. Should high-school coaches be allowed to direct kids to play more of a sport for a pay-to-play club in which they have a financial interest? Our son went from liking and respecting his high-school coach to wanting nothing to do with him as a result of him not being allowed to play a sport for nothing more than fun in-season.

Our son loved and excelled at every sport he ever tried, but he eventually felt remarkable pressure to continue to compete solely for the club team. It was at that point, when the great expectations started to emerge, that he often started to dislike the sport, or the coach in any case. He would have been much better served by a message that said, whenever you can be with this team, we value your time and effort, and your presence will help the team. Instead, he sadly felt forced to choose between sports that he loved, or used to love, before he became the target of some coaches' repeated, intense diatribes about not devoting more time to a particular sport.

He was repeatedly told by youth coaches that he "could be great" in hopes of him choosing their sport as his primary focus. Whether or not he could have been "great" depends on the definition of greatness. It is fair to say that he was unusually athletic so that he could definitely help teams win, but it was nonetheless his decision as to where he put that time and energy into achieving greatness or not.

Our son would have given everything he had to all sports he could play in a year if he was told he was valued for what he could contribute at that moment, without being handed the pamphlet about the pay-to-play version of the sport. The lectures before, during, and after the season by some coaches about inadequate commitment, or for missing one practice because of his commitment to his main pay-to-play sport, only led him to feel that he had not enough to give when he could not be in two places at the same time.

And so, instead of playing for the love of the game, he felt he had to quit some sports. Sadly, he let go of participating in some sports he really wanted to play just for the enjoyment of them. The time, drive, and desire were there; the support from the adults that ran the program, who always wanted more, was not. Some coaches, thankfully, do better, but this territory is complicated to an extent that parental involvement will likely be needed to help the young athlete navigate it successfully, keeping in mind how difficult it is for kids to assert themselves to adults, even if they are more than within their rights to do so.

If you have a multisport athlete, beware of coaches competing for the athlete's time and loyalty to their sport. Clearly some coaches are so desperate to win, to have their program dominate, or are so insecure in their sense of self that the lengths they will go to to ensure that your child stays with their sport are shocking. Deep down, these coaches know that there is nothing they can do to stop an athlete from playing another sport, or doing other activities of interest in the off-season, but if the athlete is one of the better players on the team, it is the rule rather than the exception that the pressure to commit will emerge. If a player misses one practice for a tryout for the next season in the "other sport," or if a player dares to attend the high-school-team league playoff game instead of the club team's practice, or if the player prioritizes the club team over the high-school team, the athlete is considered guilty of many irreparable personal deficiencies that will, bottom line, harm the team.

The charges against multisport child athletes at every age and level of sport they play are many and varied: not serious enough, unwilling to commit, afraid to succeed, abandoning their team responsibilities, unwilling to put in more work to succeed at the level that their talent would easily allow, selfish, stubborn, loner, and the list likely goes on from the infuriated coaches who feel their "love" for the player was unrequited. Other coaches have demanded to know, "Why should I put in the effort to help you when you don't put in the effort I say is needed to help this team?!" And so, these coaches refuse to answer skills- or tactics-related questions, decline to help with recruiting, and resolve to disallow the athlete a second more of playing time throughout the season.

What happened to young athletes playing for the love of the game? Our oldest daughter, her uncles, and her father had all played college-level Division I soccer. One stunning and baffling observation we made during her college career was that none of her teammates wanted to play pickup or indoor soccer in the off-season. She wanted to play as much as possible. Her uncle, who attended the same university and played on the men's team in the 1970s, was utterly at a loss when he learned about her teammates' apathy regarding playing in the off-season. Had soccer become nothing more than a means to get admission to college, or something to put on a résumé, after which one went through the motions of being a varsity athlete, the love of the game having been smothered long ago by the Youth Sports Industry?

If you are wondering whether your child is still playing a sport for the wrong reasons, and the consequences of play are accumulating, consider talking to some "neutral" coaches who may be recently retired or live in a different state, with no connection to your current club. Consult with your athlete's physician to see if the doctor can talk to your child. Ask for a referral to a psychologist and/or a sports psychologist to see if they can ascertain how your child feels about playing. Compare the results of these valuable opinions from coaches and professionals and see how closely they resemble what your child seems to be communicating to you. If your child still loves to play, it should be obvious. But if the child no longer loves to play, it may be very difficult for the child to tell the parents. The more the parents invest in the child's sport, the more pressure the child feels to play the sport.[27]

A Realistic Plan for Finding the Right College Match

There are countless guides published about finding the right academic college for your child, and there are countless college counselors to advise you on securing the best chances for admission at a prestigious college. We will leave that work to them. Here we will attempt to help you with what has been the most useful information we have learned along the way in guiding our three talented youth athletes, who were interested in being recruited. The following question is really the most important question of all to consider. What college is the right college for your child if for some reason his or her sports career ends? Consider the location, cost, size, academic offerings, and other interest-related opportunities that would make this college the right fit for your child.

Only then look to see if the college has a sports team that might be appropriate for your child. We know that after thirteen or more years of watching your passionate athlete compete, it is nearly impossible to imagine that your child will stop playing that sport or all sports some time in the near future. However, there are countless reasons why that near future may come sooner than you think.

What if your child gets injured during prime college recruiting time and is unable to showcase play? What if your child strongly dislikes the recruiting process and loses interest before recruitment? What if your child is cut from the college team and loses a scholarship? What if the coach who recruited your child is fired or moves on to another college during your child's time there (a far more common occurrence than you might think)?

Will your child still be able to play for the incoming coach—and want to? What if the sport's team at that college is cut due to a pandemic-related budget crisis, as numerous ones were? What if your child finds that the time commitment for a college-level sport is too much to handle while keeping up with academics? What if your child gets a fourth concussion in college and the doctor says no more? What if your child finds something else in college that captures the imagination and passion and steps away from the sport?

Many Division I players find themselves overwhelmed by the time commitment involved to do sports in college and do not enjoy the experience at all. Many quit early into the first season, and some quit before they even start the team.

There are many excellent college teams, coaches, and balanced educational-athletic environments at other colleges. These environments are often found at the D2, D3, NAIA, and NJCAA level, with the main difference being that no scholarship money is allowed to be given at the D3 levels. For many of the smaller sports, a strong D3 team may frequently beat a D1 team. No scholarship also means that D3 players may have much more time available to them in the off-season. Many colleges that fund athletic teams still try to foster the belief that your son or daughter is a student first and an athlete second and not the other way around. The job of any parent is to know the difference between the two.

The student academic support center is one place for more information, as are alumni athletes, current athletes on a team, or ones who have quit a team. Often coaches are willing to make some of these names available. No scholarship also means it is much more likely that a player's time in college is not monopolized by requirements of coaches who "own them." We have heard of D1 players required to staff a college's summer camps as unpaid volunteers, or they are not paid enough to support the cost of living in a major metropolitan area when no scholarship aid is available outside of the college's official semesters.

In addition, it appears that often, with some exceptions, the bigger the sport and its prestige at the university the lower the expectations for the student's academic performance. What good will that D1 scholarship do for the student when, after being done playing college ball, it becomes clear that making the pros is not in the cards and yet the student has invested very little in preparing for a career when the time comes to hang up the sneakers or cleats? Parents have every right to know the team's average GPA and how many players are asked to leave a team annually due to academic deficiencies. Is there a tutoring center for the athletes? Are the athletes expected to do their own work (getting an honest answer at a high-powered sports school can be a joke)? There are many fine, intelligent scholar athletes at all college-division levels of play. But the fact that institutions of higher learning need to continue making millions of dollars off of these high-level athletes is the driving priority at most institutions. If the star player fails a class, then the team might fail, and then the money might fail. Does this seem in the best interests of our student athletes?

Chapter 5

How Change Could Happen

The Youth Sports Industry is embedded in a broader societal context. There are many pieces to the puzzle so reforming the overall system could be difficult. There are also many individuals and organizations who profit from the system and others who believe that the present Youth Sports Industry is working just fine. These people and organizations will go along with reforms only if they have no choice—if they are legally required to do so, for example—or if other agents force them to change.

How could change happen? One possibility that seems unlikely in the short term may eventually happen, especially because other countries already do a much better job than the United States in this area. Perhaps down the road Americans will come to view making sports available to all youth who want to participate to be a national priority, and politicians will respond by providing the funding and governmental oversight to make this happen. This would presumably require slightly higher taxes in order to provide for the necessary infrastructure, both physical and human, to make such an initiative successful rather than just rhetorical. It is also plausible that the return on investment, such as lowered rates of obesity, juvenile delinquency, and various other benefits that reduce future spending (e.g., healthcare or incarceration costs) might exceed or substantially mitigate the required funding of greater participation in youth sports under better coaching.

In his 2008 book *Game On*, Tom Farrey quotes Tom McMillen calling for a fundamental rethinking of the sports structure in the United States. McMillen views the U.S. as an unhealthy outlier for not having something along the lines of a Ministry of Sport, which so many other nation-states have.[28] A retired pro basketball player who went on to serve in Congress and later as chairman of the board of directors of the President's Foundation on Sports, Physical Fitness, and Nutrition, McMillen is especially well-positioned to have a broader view of what is lacking in youth-sports infrastructure here in the United States.

There is a longstanding lineage among some Americans of a fear of "big government," a pedigree that seems as prominent today as ever. Nonetheless, one can imagine a time down the road when a well-managed Department of Sports at the federal level regulates youth sports across the country in a way that results in a much better system than the one we have at present. Imagine the day when all parents with children interested in playing sports would need to check before enlisting their child in a program to verify that this specific sports program has the Department of Sports stamp of approval for carrying out youth sports in a safe, developmentally appropriate manner.

Parents would come to be so acculturated to look for that stamp of approval that almost any organization that had not earned it would be driven out of existence. Add into the equation funding for youth sports that would make participation possible by all who want to take part and the United States would have reached the standard that already exists in much of the developed world. We are not imagining some utopia in youth sports but rather steps that would bring the United States up to the standard of numerous other nations in this arena such as Australia. If achieving such a goal needs further justification, one can easily point out that Australia consistently hauls home far more medals at Olympic competitions than its population would seem to justify.

Proponents of the system that privileges the market often want to extend the market to as many areas of society as possible, but it is by no means clear that the market system suits all areas of society. Other pluralistic democracies that also have capitalist economies see youth sports as an area that should not be left to the market but rather as an area where it is necessary for the government to step in to provide something approaching equal opportunity. The system that leaves more and more to the market benefits a particular class disproportionately at the expense of the majority of individuals. But this book is about the Youth Sports Industry, not the overall political economic system.

Concerned individuals can and should lobby their elected representatives to invest in and regulate youth sports in a way that would extend better and safer opportunities to more and more kids rather than, for example, developing mega-sized luxurious facilities to be rented by clubs that cater to the socioeconomic elite. At a more collective level, national sports bodies could lobby more assertively for changes along these lines, too, as could other civic groups. A combination of education and lobbying is required. The Aspen Institute is already active in both of these areas through its Project Play initiative.

In August of 2021, the Aspen Institute, through a drafting committee drawn from six major American organizations dedicated to human rights and sports policy, formulated a Children's Bill of Rights in Sports.[29] We quote these eight rights to highlight how basic and fundamental they are, and yet these rights clearly need to be developed and protected in a country as seemingly "privileged" as the United States. Project Play's eight children's sports' rights include: "The right to play sports, the right to safe and healthy environments, the right to qualified program leaders, the right to developmentally appropriate play, the right to share in the planning and delivery of their activities, the right to equal opportunity for personal growth, the right to be treated with dignity, and the right to enjoy themselves." This codification of children's fundamental rights in sports is simple and clear. How we go about achieving these rights will depend on our ability to recognize the urgency for change across multiple societal systems.

Many ideas that initially seem farfetched eventually gain social traction and then political backing, but progress toward those goals can be a long slog. According to the Overton Window, which theorizes how societal ideas eventually gain enough of a grip to be made into policy by elected officials, it is by no means out of the question that greater support for inclusive youth sports could gain this traction. So better to start now or the goal will always be in the far future. The overarching goal of these reforms should be to provide more opportunities for youth to participate in sports, not to protect vested interests in the Youth Sports Industry.

Colleges and Their Recruiting and Admissions Policies

What if, starting with the next admissions cycle, all American institutions of higher education announced that they would no longer offer preferential admission to athletes? Presumably, the Youth Sports Industry as it presently stands would soon collapse. Rick Eckstein's 2017 book *How College Athletics are Hurting Girls' Sports* provides support for this premise.[30] The necessity of this critical college athletics–linked reform to repair youth sports cannot be underestimated by those dedicated to vital current reforms. The so-called return on investment that so many families are looking for includes dreams of nurturing a professional athlete, but the goal of preferential admission to an elite college is nonetheless what drives the system. Parents who are in the know about obtaining and maintaining privilege can tell you, even when their kids are still young, about athletic recruitment and scholarships at the university level. One set of parents from our children's high school spoke openly of their plan to use soccer to get their son into Yale, after which he would quit the soccer team. The notion that this kid would play at any level in college was so removed from reality that the plan proved a fantasy, but it speaks to how much youth sports has become a mechanism to gain admission.

Although there are families for whom an athletic scholarship is a ticket to an otherwise seemingly inaccessible college education, the goal for many families who are involved in pay-to-play sports is first and foremost admission to an elite-level university to keep status and privilege intact. Such elite economic and social privilege has always been passed down from one generation to the next, but only recently has youth sports come to play such an important role in this area. Institutions of higher education have become complicit in accentuating the role of sports in helping the elite maintain its socioeconomic status. There does not appear to be some master plan followed by institutions of higher education, but nonetheless most college sports play a role in replicating the elite rather than providing opportunities for social mobility.

Such a dramatic and immediate curtailing by higher education of preferential admission for athletes seems unlikely. It is probably no more likely than Americans suddenly achieving a consensus, not in rhetoric but in reality, that would include the necessary funding for a Department of Sports, which would provide the opportunity for all kids to play sports regularly. In the meantime, how could American colleges and universities be pushed to take action that would rein in the worst excesses of the Youth Sports Industry and also be pushed to rethink preferential admission for athletes?

This is not a book about the lucrative grafting of sports and higher education in the United States, which enriches so many actors. Other books have taken up that topic. But a start would be to ask some tough questions of colleges and universities about specific practices that do not seem to accord with the image they promote about themselves in many areas, such as serving as an engine for social mobility.

Putting aside the cases of men's DI football, basketball, and to some extent baseball, let's focus on the remaining sports, including all women's sports. There is so much money to be made through college football and men's basketball that there is a vast system in place that searches almost every nook and cranny of the United States as well as beyond the national borders for talent. The fact that Major League Baseball has a vast infrastructure for identifying talent helps with the sorting for those who attend college. Some of this talent for these "money sports" definitely comes from lower socioeconomic classes. Whether or not the K–12 system has done right by these student-athletes in terms of preparing them to succeed academically in college is a different question, but these sports do play a role in providing a shot at college to young athletes who otherwise would not have a chance.

This is much less the case for other sports at the DI level, however. In *Game On*, Farrey has this to say about who is playing college sports: "[A] survey by the U.S. Department of Education debunked the notion of college sports as a tool of broad social uplift. Tracking students from the eighth grade through college, it found that children with a high socioeconomic status [those in the top 25 percent on a measure that considers their parents' occupations, education, and income] were 10 times as likely to play Division I sports as those with low socioeconomic status [those in the bottom 25 percent]."[31] The situation is no less, and very possibly more, pronounced at the DII level and the DIII level, which constitutes the largest group of NCAA schools.

There are also many college teams that operate under national bodies other than the NCAA. Anyone who believes that sports, in fact, provides a door into colleges for minority and disadvantaged athletes should look at the makeup of college fencing, squash, and water-polo teams, just to mention a few examples. With niche sports, preferential admission of athletes is far more likely to benefit socioeconomically elite families than minority and disadvantaged ones. The Mellon Foundation study College and Beyond evidences data that "college-recruited athletes are up to four times more likely to be admitted to prestigious schools than legacies or members of underrepresented demographic groups."[32] But why exactly should athletes get preferential admission? Does the rapid expansion of colleges offering lacrosse as a varsity sport go beyond the simple growth of this sport at the youth level? At this point, lacrosse remains largely a sport of the socioeconomic elite, making it especially attractive for colleges to add it as a varsity sport.

As we have seen in the Varsity Blues scandal, some socioeconomically advantaged families will stop at nothing to provide their children with a leg up. Even as these families try to help their kids get preferential admission for their athletics by purchasing all the coaching and travel to tournaments that money can buy, some parents within this elite think nothing of using highly dubious means to leverage the Americans with Disabilities Act (ADA) to get their children diagnosed with a supposed learning disability. If such a diagnosis can be finagled, these children must be provided extra time to take tests, including the standardized tests that still factor in admissions at many institutions of higher education. But with sports being a clear path to admission to an elite university, the socioeconomic elite spares no expense.

DIII sporting contests rarely are featured on nationally televised broadcasts the way that DI football and basketball games are, but it would be a mistake to underestimate the cutthroat competition to gain admission to Amherst, Pomona, Williams, Swarthmore, and similar DIII schools and just how high the percentage of athletes is at these small liberal-arts colleges. The difficulty of obtaining admission into elite American colleges and universities has grown by leaps and bounds between 1990 and 2019. Yet, one group has maintained the highest likelihood of admission compared to its peers, above even minority candidates and legacies during that time: student-athletes. Between the years 1976 and 1999, student-athletes' admissions doubled from a 23 percent greater likelihood to a 48 percent greater likelihood of being admitted than their nonathlete peers.[33]

High-school student-athletes are a force to be reckoned with. The high-school student-athletes' academic and athletic talents might mean that a nonathlete's spot at the entry door to their parents' adult world of privilege could be stolen away. So, as the saying goes, if you cannot beat them, join them. Get your kids into athletics, if possible into a niche sport such as fencing that offers a better path to preferential admission. In a broad-range survey, the percentage of student-athletes recruited and admitted to these top-tier universities was reported as falling anywhere in the range of 1 percent of the overall student body at the University of California Irvine to an astonishing 36 percent at Williams College,[34] one of the most elite small liberal-arts colleges that competes at the DIII level.

Just one generation ago, wealthy parents, when thinking about college for their child, might never have spent a moment thinking about what sport their child should take up to gain admission and which elite sports club provided the best return on investment in this endeavor. Fast forward to today and some of these parents employ an army of Youth Sports Industry professionals in hopes of covering all the best angles of access to the elite colleges and universities. This includes parents who may have spent their own childhoods in foreign countries where sports participation was often considered a leisure-time pursuit best left to those who would not make it in their country's world of financially successful adults, excepting a few star athletes. As immigrant parents learn the ways of American higher education, would they quickly understand the importance of sports participation to gaining admission to college if it were not so consequential? Word of this system has spread even to the elite outside the United States.

Institutions of higher education should be required to align their policies with their rhetoric. If they claim to be engines of social mobility, then why the relatively new emphasis on athletics as such an important factor for admission? The empirical evidence shows that such policies basically allow colleges to select athletes from a pool of the socioeconomic elite that can not only pay full tuition but also are a likely source of donations.

The recruiting budgets that most coaches have do not help the situation. When we were making the rounds of colleges with our second daughter, we heard the women's soccer coach at Williams College, a tremendously successful program that has won national championships, describe her recruiting budget. It was basically enough for her to make one recruiting trip annually, typically to a tournament that offered her the opportunity to see the greatest number of players that she might otherwise not encounter in light of Williams's location in Massachusetts. Such a minuscule recruiting budget is more the rule than most people realize.

High-school girls who express interest in playing soccer at Williams College—and most every other college in the United States—are unsurprisingly told to attend one of its ID camps. In fact, many coaches have an email auto-reply that directs high-school kids to sign up for the next ID camp. That is the only initial reply the interested high-school student typically gets from many college coaches.

The bottom line is that a high percentage of American families cannot afford to send their high-school athlete to even one ID camp much less return to one school's ID camps over and over or to take part in the circuit to attract the attention of a coach. The ID-camp circuit caters almost entirely to the socioeconomic elite and is so thoroughly estranged from the supposed mission of American higher education to serve as an engine for social mobility that it is baffling why college and university leaders accept this status quo.

Eliminating the ID-camp system entirely seems unlikely, but how could it be reformed? First, colleges and universities need to closely regulate their ID camps, which reflect on the reputations of these institutions. One can only imagine the fury that would be directed by a college administration at a faculty member who staged some sort of summer academic ID camp in the name of the university that dangled the hook of possible preferential admission (especially if there were zero chance that most or even all of the participants would gain admission), so why are coaches allowed to run amok with ID camps? Success in reforming one area can have a ripple effect.

Any parents who have sent their high-school athlete to even one ID camp have no doubt noticed that although the ID camp is promoted using the name of one or more colleges, payment is almost always made to a Limited Liability Corporation that is owned by a member of the coaching staff. Why is this the case? If the ID camps are claiming that they are being offered by, for example, Harvard, why is it that the payment does not go through Harvard? If the payment went to Harvard, then Harvard would feel more responsibility for regulating the ID camps that attract participants by leveraging its name.

There are some ways that ID camps could be better regulated. First, every ID camp should be required to provide statistics on how many players as a percentage of the overall who attended actually gained a spot on the team by attending an ID camp offered by that college in the previous five years. In many cases, the statistics would show that zero high-school athletes got a spot on a team. There are prestigious colleges shooting for national championships that have already lined up their recruits from the pool of junior-national-team players as well as international players long before the coaches sponsor ID camps. So why do the administrations at these colleges allow these ID camps to continue to be held?

Old-fashioned statistics would reveal that in some cases, perhaps even many cases, ID camps are nothing more than a way to take advantage of hopeful families in order to pad the salaries of the coaching staff. If the colleges and universities were more involved in overseeing these ID camps, it is likely they would be quite uncomfortable with the fact that many ID camps are trading on the prestige of the college's name.

Assuming that the ID-camp system is not going away any time soon, one reform would be to require coaches to make attendance by invitation only and to strictly limit the number of spots available. High-school athletes interested in a college team would still be permitted to contact the coaching staff to express interest in attending an ID camp, but registration would not be first come, first served.

If ID camps are to in fact become legitimate ways for coaches to evaluate players, why not require that the coaches do a basic level of scouting before admitting a high-school athlete to an ID camp? And why not limit the total number of ID-camp spots that colleges can offer in a given year in order to force coaches to vet each player carefully, including in the area of academics, before accepting their overture to attend an ID camp?

Admissions offices do pre-reads of athletes to determine if they are likely to be admitted. The same could be required for high-school athletes wanting to attend ID camps to see if there is an academic match before being admitted. If the coaches determine that there is a realistic chance of that player winning a spot on the college team, which would include being academically qualified, to justify the time and expense of a student-athlete attending an ID camp, then and only then should that player be invited. The NCAA could also take action in this area rather than leaving it to individual institutions.

In addition, if colleges were serious about living up to their commitment to make their institutions open to individuals from all class backgrounds, pressure could be exerted on them to offer financial aid to prospects who could not attend these camps otherwise. If the NCAA has a regulation forbidding this, then it, too, would have to be reformed. After all, it is more than a little duplicitous for colleges to condone a recruiting system for athletes that fundamentally favors the socioeconomic elite even while portraying themselves as engines of social mobility. There are other ways to accomplish the same goal. Coaches could be provided with recruiting budgets to be used specifically for finding athletes from families who otherwise would not have the means to pursue the typical route to admission to one of these colleges.

Making ID camps selective would also, when it comes to a college-soccer ID camp under the current system, for example, eliminate the way in which teammates a player is randomly assigned during the course of the ID camp influences what that player can show to the coaches. If a player is grouped with recreational soccer players who interpreted the ID camp as just another summer camp (and, in order to attract large numbers of paying participants, many ID camps use blurred language that suggests that the camp has a developmental or recreational purpose too, rather than being geared exclusively toward recruiting), it is next to impossible to show well.

At one ID camp, our son ended up being placed on a team mostly with eighth graders, who both in terms of physical development and soccer skills were not in the same league as a twelfth grader, making it difficult for the older players on the team to attract the attention of coaches since the unevenness of the team made functioning as a unit next to impossible.

Our oldest daughter remembers vividly that when she attended the Dartmouth College ID camp in the summer of 2013, the coaches, even before the camp began, projected the likely recruits and put them all on one team, to which all the other teams could not possibly measure up, making it almost impossible for those players to be taken seriously. If the coaches are going to follow this kind of protocol, why did they accept the other players at the camp other than for the obvious?

At present, the ID-camp circuit is reminiscent of the days before the U.S. had a Federal Drug Administration. ID camps are touted similarly to the way medicines were advertised in the pre-FDA era, by playing on hope and desperation. But just as many medicines in those days had no positive effects, and some were harmful, the overall effectiveness of the ID-camp circuit in terms of matching high-school athletes with colleges, compared to the remarkable amount of money families spend on it, is dismal to damaging.

No doubt many college coaches would like to have their unrestricted recruiting budget increased, but this would be a cautionary tale. Enabling coaches to attend more tournaments would lessen their dependence on ID camps, but enabling college coaches, including at the DIII level, to attend more showcase tournaments, ECNL and otherwise, would simply provide them more opportunities to observe players who largely come from the socioeconomically elite. It does not get to the root of the problem, which is that the monetary bar separating those who can participate in pay-to-play, including attending travel tournaments regularly, from those who cannot is already so high that in most sports the chance to gain preferential admission on the basis of athletics is fundamentally tilted toward the socioeconomic elite.

So this returns us to the question of how to change the fundamental system—to get colleges to rethink the entire process of recruiting. How does an educational institution keep the system open to individuals from non-elite backgrounds to keep open their hope for mobility? The present system of preferential admission for athletes takes refuge in claims of resting on merit, but does it rest on merit? That depends on the definition of merit.

If a young student-athlete, through tutoring by coaches and competition made possible only by the wealth of parents, can become a good enough tennis player to participate in a DIII program, then that player may gain preferential admission to an elite college. College administrators often justify special admission for kids who excel in extracurriculars by pointing out that these students tend to transfer the life lessons they learned by excelling in extracurriculars to their careers and other areas of adult life.

The problem is the limited number of kids who ever have a shot at such preferential admission. Certain colleges do provide admission and also financial aid to a small percentage of students from backgrounds that are not privileged and who would not be able to attend otherwise, so they are making some efforts to level the field. Colleges and universities advertise themselves positively and justify their tax-free status by claiming that they are a good for society, in no small part because they provide opportunity. And in many ways, they are good for society. But they need to align their rhetoric with reality.

For example, why should athletes be provided with preferential admission to a college such as Swarthmore, to name just one college among many at the DIII level? Is this a societal good? Players on such college teams often have a more fun college experience and likely learn some life lessons. But at the same time, is a societal good being accomplished by having a college soccer team comprised largely of the socioeconomic elite?

College administrators may not be entirely aware of the problems with ID camps, but there is no way that they are unaware that a disproportionate percentage of athletes in most sports come from the socioeconomic elite and increasingly from a worldwide socioeconomic elite as families outside of the United States have caught on to the role that sports plays in gaining admission to the American system of higher education. It seems as though institutions of higher education have found a way to hide behind a façade of athletic merit in order to justify preferential admission to members of the socioeconomic elite, which of course serves their own purposes.

According to the present model under which American colleges operate, courting families from the elite has the same compounded value that it does for the pay-to-play clubs. First, these families can pay full tuition for their child to attend college. Second, the parents are often already donors to the college, or they will become donors, sometimes to grease the admissions process and in other cases once their child is admitted. Third, the children of the elite (in line to inherit wealth) are more likely to become donors to their alma mater down the road, particularly if they remember how much fun they had at college being on a sports team or even just being a spectator at major sporting events.

Something would presumably give if the colleges were subjected to questioning along the lines of: "You portray your institution as an engine for social mobility, but in most sports you are stacking the cards dramatically in favor of the socioeconomic elite. How does this accord with the statement on your website that portrays your institution as promoting opportunity for all? If all this concentrated wealth in the form of endowments serves mainly to replicate the elite, then why should it not be taxed?" Colleges, especially in the elite echelon, need to be pushed to admit what purpose preferential admission for athletes really serves, which could make them uncomfortable enough that it might lead to change.

It is also possible that by pointing out guilt by association, institutions of higher education would alter their practices to discourage other ills of the Youth Sports Industry such as the year-round practice and competition schedules that result in overuse injuries, and the tournament circuit, which largely encourages, indeed requires, high-school and even junior-high-school students to miss school regularly. Incredible as it may seem, if the NCAA or a number of institutions of higher education were simply to forbid coaches from recruiting at pay-to-play tournaments and the like that require players to miss school, that alone would lead to dramatic reforms in the pay-to-play system.

Such a reform would rein in the developmentally suspect tournament system significantly for it would be next to impossible to stage many tournaments outside of the summer months. Other than during the few long weekends that result from federal holidays or during winter and spring breaks, it is simply not possible, outside of summer months, to stage a tournament that includes teams flying in for games that would not require the missing of school.

Gaining admission at increasingly competitive elite colleges and universities via youth sports has itself become a societal problem, resulting in many crumpled youth bodies and minds. Is that coveted spot for admission by a privileged athlete to a prestigious university really worth the emotional, physical, financial, and social toll it often exacts on the athletes and their families? And what cost to the rest of our non-athlete applicant youth and to the larger society are we willing to pay? If youth sports is to return to a healthier, less destructive, and more inclusive form, comprehensive change is a must.

State and Federal Legislation

State legislatures as well as their federal counterparts regularly take action to protect children, including in the area of sports. The history of sports-concussion policies and laws have changed dramatically in the past fifteen years as the result of legislative action, so it is by no means a pipe dream that legislative action could reform the Youth Sports Industry. The concern over concussions has swept the nation, and we hope that the overall overuse epidemic and other ills of the pay-to-play system are the next to receive attention. The story of how legislatures intervened in the area of concussions provides a model for how they might effect change in other areas.

In 2009, the state of Washington passed the Zachary Lystedt Law to require concussion management in youth athletics, specifically to forbid coaches and others from playing any further an athlete suspected of having sustained a concussion until that athlete is cleared by a medical professional. Sadly, this law resulted from the sort of tragedy that we hope can be avoided in the area of overuse injuries. After the initial law was passed by the state of Washington, the remaining 49 state-level legislatures soon passed similar legislation. We would like to see movement by legislatures before, hypothetically, Suzanne's Law is passed, named after a teenage girl who will spend the rest of her life with knees that simply could not be fully repaired after multiple overuse injuries.

What is likely to result in action by legislatures in the area of overuse injuries? All of the actors who are familiar with the problem—the health-insurance companies that pay to repair the young athletes, the secondary-school administrators all too familiar with seeing a shocking number of their student athletes felled for an entire year, coaches in favor of a return to sanity, and especially medical professionals who see the overuse injuries firsthand—need to push this problem into the public's consciousness, so much so that legislators cannot ignore it. It is, admittedly, a tricky area, because legislators would need to step in and regulate pay-to-play clubs where a subset of parents demand more and more practices and games.

So, we are calling also in part for regulation of the parents, which will no doubt enrage some. But legislatures have been willing to venture into this arena before to prevent other forms of parental negligence or abuse. Yes, we call upon legislators to define overuse injuries as a form of neglect or even abuse and to step in to demand that responsible parties change their ways or face sanctions. Sometimes it only takes one state legislature to get the ball rolling.

Of course legislatures, including at the national level, could go further. Congress could not only require national sports federations to develop best practices but could also provide a legal framework whereby any sports organization that did not follow these best practices would lose its tax-free status. Better still, Congress could establish and fund a Ministry of Sports that could address so many of the problems.

Legislatures could also take up the matter of preferential admission of athletes by institutions of higher education. Though this is far less likely in reference to the overuse-injury epidemic, it is not out of the question. State legislatures could ban preferential admission for athletes by their state universities. Practices of private institutions are more difficult to regulate but not beyond the purview of Congress. In fact, private institutions of higher education are more under the control of the federal government than most people realize for one major reason.

Almost all private colleges and universities accept grants and other forms of funding from the federal government, which in some cases runs into the hundreds of millions, especially for any university that includes a medical college. The federal government can require and has repeatedly required that all institutions of higher education accepting federal grant monies obey federal law in other areas. This could easily extend to admissions policies. If preferential admission for athletes by elite universities is simply a way to keep the donation dollars rolling in, then institutions of higher education have some explaining to do. In recent years, increasing attention has been focused by Congress on the concentrations of wealth, in the form of endowments, that various colleges and universities enjoy, with mostly tax-free status. In 2017, Congress passed a law that started to tax college and university endowments for the first time, even if at paltry rates, but these rates could be raised. Just the threat by Congress that the tax rates on endowments would be raised for institutions of higher education that do not cease preferential admission for athletes (and for legacies for that matter) could be enough to spur action in this area.

In 2023, the Supreme Court ruled against the use of race in college admissions in reference to *Students for Fair Admission v President and Fellows of Harvard*. What is curious about this case is its singular focus on race when so many other nonacademic factors go into college admissions. For example, discrimination toward female applicants, who tend to have superior academic records, by the elite schools, which seek gender balance in each admitted class, is rampant. So why not a lawsuit about that, or about the fact that "legacies," applicants with a relative who attended the college, get preferential admission?

In reference to this book, why not a lawsuit challenging why athletes should get preferential admission to college over those who have excelled academically. This recent Supreme Court case directs attention toward one factor in college admissions while ignoring all the other nonacademic factors that feature in college admissions.

National Sports Organizations

A Department of Sports could reform most of what is bad about the Youth Sports Industry, but until that time there are ways to get much closer to accomplishing certain goals. First, if various national bodies that govern sports in the United States, such as the United States Soccer Federation, compressed the gap of how often they look the other way even as their affiliates engage in practices contrary to what is considered appropriate for developing youth athletes, that would be meaningful. It would also be meaningful if we could reach the stage whereby any youth club that did not have the official stamp of approval from the national sports federation, which itself was a model for how to undertake youth sports, would be considered a no-go for parents. This would drive noncompliant clubs out of business and much of what is wrong with the Youth Sports Industry could be curtailed.

Although there are exemplary national organizations such as USA Swimming, in other cases national federations would have to clean up their acts in order to earn the necessary respect for their guidance to have meaning. There is agreement among the better youth-soccer coaches in the United States that the focus on winning from the earliest ages is in fact counterproductive in terms of development. But by sponsoring a national championship for club teams at young ages, United States Youth Soccer in fact contributes to the problem rather than sets an example and demands others follow it. Why? New leadership is needed or more time is needed for the leadership of Cindy Parlow Cone, elected president of the United States Soccer Federation in 2020, to trickle down.

Why does the United States Soccer Federation do nothing even while one of its youth affiliates, in this case United States Youth Soccer, sponsors tournaments that are contrary to developmental models that enjoy a broad consensus worldwide? Before many national sporting organizations would reach a point of commanding respect, they would need to look at themselves in the mirror and undertake some reforms that will likely have various agents of the Youth Sports Industry screaming. It is not enough for the United States Soccer Federation and similar sports bodies simply to focus on the national teams.

Assuming a time when enlightened national federations with the will and cachet to regulate the youth programs across the country has been reached, what would youth-sports clubs have to do to receive the stamp of approval from the national organization? They would have to prove that they were in compliance with a framework of best practices that would include the bill of rights for youth athletes. The framework of best practices would cover every area of youth sports such as the representative ones that follow.

An empowered national federation would limit the number of games and practices that are permitted on a weekly/monthly/annual basis for different age groups, with significant breaks when the kids neither practice nor play games, with severe penalties for non-observance. It would require clubs to devote themselves to encouraging wide participation and hopefully kick in some funding. It would require that boards of directors for the clubs operate under standardized best practices for boards; for example, board members would be barred from making or receiving gifts to or from the coaching staff. It would also define best practices as extending to a ban on coaches accepting gifts of any kind or of a value more than $5 from families whose children they coach. Coaches would also be banned from offering private tutoring sessions to any players on their teams and perhaps even in their clubs. In other words, all situations that present conflicts of interest would be forbidden.

An empowered national federation could also require and enforce that every coach in the organization receive training in children's cognitive, emotional, and physical norms for their specific sport across a developmental span. These training guidelines would be required to be readily available on the sport-specific national-governing-body websites. A promising recent development, SafeSport, a trans-sport national youth-athlete-protection organization established in 2017 could extend its mandates to areas such as overuse injuries.

In the United States, SafeSport is sanctioned and empowered by an act of Congress called the Protecting Young Victims From Sexual Abuse and Safe Sport Authorization Act. This organization is charged with "ending sexual, physical, and emotional abuse on behalf of athletes everywhere."[35] SafeSport's mandate includes the provision of training, resources, and education to help prevent child-athlete abuse. In addition, it has a 24/7 abuse reporting hotline and provides investigations to assist state and local law enforcement to resolve abuse allegations within every national governing body and the United States Olympic and Paralympic sports organization.

SafeSport conducts annual audits to ensure compliance with child-abuse-prevention laws in all sports organizations. It is empowered to provide sanctions for failure to comply with these federal laws to the individual adults connected with youth-sports organizations, ranging from sanctions to permanent ineligibility for future participation within sports organizations at any level. The SafeSport agency's experts can provide invaluable guidance into the development of new legislation to help close the gaps in abuse prevention. For example, the 2018 Protecting Young Victims From Sexual Abuse and Safe Sport Authorization Act helped close gaps between states with differing mandated reporter laws by extending the mandatory child-abuse reporting requirements to include coaches and other adults affiliated with all national governing bodies or other amateur sports organizations.

SafeSport was created due to the horrifying levels of abuse that continue to occur in our nation's youth-sports organizations, from the recreational level up through the Olympic level. It is a powerful example of a national organization that has been granted the legal scope and power to protect youth from what is otherwise a grossly unregulated sports system, thoroughly vulnerable to the abuses of adults from financial exploitation to physical, emotional, and sexual abuse of the youth athletes these adults are charged to serve and protect. We need more of the national governing associations for the individual sports to provide similar leadership in these areas.

What if sports clubs were required to provide easy access to a listing of publicly available information on any coaches and affiliated adults about whom an abuse investigation had been initiated during the course of their tenure with that club? This information is spread largely by word of mouth, but after about a two-year cycle, the collective parental knowledge of what occurred and by whom has been lost. Although there are registries of adults who have been convicted of child-abuse-related crimes, even when searching the name of a known coach offender, the information was not listed in our state but rather a different state in which the coach now lived.

In an effort to protect the remaining rights of convicted offenders, or in an effort to protect the winning potential of that sports club or athlete, countless "pass the trash" and "why weren't we informed by the parties that knew" stories continue to occur in the next vulnerable youth-sports community until the offenses grow too serious and too numerous to miss. Clubs could help protect their youth-family consumers from abuse by making easily accessible public information about problems that have occurred in the past with adults who have been affiliated with their organizations. When a mandatory report has been made, and founded, by matter of course this information should be provided to parents, coaches, and club administrators. It should be catalogued and easily accessible to a future club when doing a reference check on these adults looking for their next landing place. This mandate to share the information could prevent abusive sports-affiliated adults from skating under the radar of the next vulnerable youth-athlete organization.

For every defect of the Youth Sports Industry, a regulation is imaginable, including in areas not as dramatic as sexual and physical abuse. For example, if neither the NCAA nor individual institutions of higher education are willing to forbid their coaches from recruiting at tournaments that require kids to miss school, then the national sports federations could withhold the stamp of approval from any club that continues to attend these tournaments. How could the national federations address the overuse injury epidemic? Many national federations, United States Youth Soccer included, have in fact long ago codified safe-practice and game schedules for each of the age groups.

It is a question of enforcement. Clubs not abiding by the safe-practice and game schedules should not only be denied the stamp of approval, but they also should be singled out for additional negative attention. National federations could deny entry into regional and national competitions at all ages to any club that does not abide by the required practice and game schedule. For that matter, the state sports federations could deny them entry into the state competitions. That would get the attention of the clubs, which desperately want to be able to tout success at the state, regional, and national level on their websites as recruiting tools.

National federations could also require pay-to-play clubs to keep track of how many of their players experience serious injuries, such as ACL tears and the like, and make this information clearly available on their websites. This is an area where pay-to-play clubs have been able to almost entirely "externalize" a cost for which they are largely responsible in many cases. At present, health-insurance companies and families pay for the costs of repairing overuse injuries, whereas clubs conveniently pay not a penny, so there is little incentive for clubs to change their practices.

It is similar to the case of polluters before there were regulations in this area. Does anyone want to return to the era when a factory could dump its effluent in the river and let others suffer the consequences even as the owners enjoyed high profits? This is basically what is happening now in terms of pay-to-play clubs and overuse injuries. The next time some club representative sings the praises of year-round training and hints that such a rigorous training schedule is the only way to get that coveted spot on a college team, parents should directly confront that club official with questions about whether the club's insurance extends to covering the costs of overuse injuries. Pressure from outside is likely the only way to get them to change their practices in this area.

National federations, once they have earned the position of respect that makes it dangerous for clubs to cross them, may have to play hardball along the way, publicly shaming pay-to-play clubs that continue with particularly egregious practices. It is easy to imagine that the national federations and the clubs will need additional nudging from the legislatures to take action in various areas. Some of the courageous national federations, in spite of their financial reliance on major sponsors, might nonetheless curtail the utterly nonsensical practice of requiring that teams as young as U-9 purchase expensive, professional uniform kits, just the sort of practice that contributes to the exclusivity that is one of the most significant problems that requires reform.

The defects of the Youth Sports Industry outlined in this book are not secrets to many individuals who have observed the system. A massive study by experts is not required to understand what is wrong. Rather, what is required is the will to change it from the sectors of society that could require and enable change.

Healthcare Professionals

Youth-sports injuries may not be a society-wide youth-injury epidemic simply because the majority of youth cannot afford pay-to-play, but it nonetheless should be considered an epidemic of preventable injuries among the millions of athletes who do participate. What if sports-medicine doctors, pediatric primary-care doctors, mental-health professionals, trainers, and physical therapists, among others, organized to develop and promote injury-prevention standards that were required by legislation to be implemented by national and state sports-governing bodies? These sport-specific standards would be required to be enforced by youth-sports organizations, both private and public, and failure to comply would leave them liable.

In fact, attempts to begin the process of developing sport-specific injury-prevention recommendations have been in place for over a decade. An article by J.S. Brenner in the journal *Pediatrics* (2007)[36] summarizes nine steps of guidance for the medical clinician to help youth athletes avoid injuries, overtraining, and burnout. Most of this advice is directed toward athletes and their parents to encourage rest, to define maximum increments of total weekly training time, to avoid overtraining, to designate time periods off from the sport, and to limit participation to only one team per season. One specific guideline suggests the clinician "convey special caution to parents with younger athletes who participate in multi-game tournaments in short periods of time."[37] But if no one is mandating that the sports clubs comply with these medical standards, how many clubs will enforce them and how many families will challenge the clubs who ignore them, especially when the family views the club as holding the means to an athletic-based college admission or scholarship?

One collaborative professional organization named STOP (Sports Trauma and Overuse Prevention) Sports Injuries was founded in 2007 by the American Orthopedic Society for Sports Medicine. In 2009, it was joined by seven other professional organizations—the American Academy of Pediatrics, the American Academy of Orthopedic Surgeons, the National Athletic Trainers Association, the American Medical Society for Sports Medicine, SAFE Kids USA, the Pediatric Orthopedic Society of America, and the Sports Physical Therapy Section.[38] This is a weighty list of participants organized and unified around the common goal of stopping youth-sports injuries to "keep kids in the game for life." The STOP Sports Injuries website describes its primary purpose thusly:

"The comprehensive public-outreach program focuses on the importance of sports safety—specifically relating to overuse and trauma injuries. The initiative not only raises awareness and provides education on injury reduction but also highlights how playing safe and smart can enhance and extend a child's athletic career, improve teamwork, reduce obesity rates, and create a lifelong love of exercise and healthy activity. Our message underscores the problems of overuse and trauma and emphasizes the expertise of our coalition of experts."

This organization is so admirable, yet we have never seen any STOP flyers or brochures distributed by sports leagues, schools, or club teams. STOP's website with information for coaches and parents has never been introduced at any of the mandatory beginning-of-the-season club-wide team meetings. What if each youth-sports organization was required to have health professionals speak at these mandatory beginning-of-the-year meetings? Although some of the pay-to-play teams our children participated in did attempt to address injury prevention through proper warmups, the consistent implementation of these injury-prevention efforts varied greatly from week to week, sport to sport, coach to coach, and team to team. The STOP organization attempts to disseminate the information at a grassroots level, but clubs do not seem to be in the business of promoting its practices.

What incentives do these clubs have to follow the recommendations? Currently, none. But what if the clubs and teams were held accountable by sports-governing bodies to enforce these standards or risk losing their certifications and ability to participate in any of the state or national sports-governing bodies' tournaments without that certification? What if the leagues, clubs, and school-based teams were all required to report their injury rates each season to a medical organization assigned to track their successful injury-prevention outcomes from season to season and report to the national sports-governing bodies their findings? What if a club's ability to obtain an insurance policy depended on an injury rate that could not be exceeded without its premiums rising or having its application to renew the policy refused? Do we need a few successful lawsuits against pay-to-play clubs to hold them accountable for overuse injuries to motivate clubs to change their practices?

Another obstacle is that all parents do not want practices to change. One of the best efforts to avoid overuse injuries we observed was at a local Portland-area club-baseball organization called AIM (Athletes in Motion). Its directors and coaches worked diligently to follow the sport-specific medically recommended guidelines on youth-baseball-player pitch counts and rest times by age. What we learned firsthand was that this was an unpopular effort in the eyes of some "win now or we will pull our kids from the team" parents.

These parents' outrage needed to be assuaged, but the endless email and phone-call complaints from them to coaches would only cease temporarily after a mandatory parent meeting the evening after less-than-great results at a weekend tournament. The irate parents refused to accept any reason that it could be advisable or acceptable for the best pitcher not to keep pitching, even when the team was already losing by nine runs. The coaches were steadfastly trying to prevent injuries to their middle-school players, but the must-win-now parents could not and would not accept this plan. To be clear, it is a subgroup of parents who are driving this insanity, although most pay-to-play clubs promote the year-round, more-is-better model. But even pay-to-play clubs have to respond to the concussion legislation previously outlined, a reminder that change is possible.

The type of legislation followed by the implementation of new policies to protect youth athletes from Traumatic Brain Injuries (TBI) could certainly be applied to protect youth athletes from overuse injuries. A collaboration between medical professionals, sports trainers, legislatures, sports organizations, coaches, and parents alike to prevent overuse injuries could most certainly be replicated. The area of overuse injuries is arguably more ambiguous and thus more complex than the case of TBI, and professionals and eventually legislatures would be required to develop, circulate, and enforce sport-specific regulations regarding what amount and type of physical use constituted overuse and for which athlete body type. But it is a worthy goal nonetheless. The enforcement of overuse-prevention protocols would result in a youth-sports-culture sea change, reforming the current "win and develop the next superstar now" mentality of the Youth Sports Industry.

There is considerable variability across local youth-sports clubs and organizations regarding the efforts they require of their coaches and players to address and prevent overuse. Appropriately resting youth athletes might mean removing a team's "superstar" in the biggest moment of the biggest game or tournament of the season. Appropriate overuse prevention might mean taking "valuable practice time" to require that the group do appropriate warmup and stretching exercises before every practice and game.

Recent attempts to reduce soccer-related concussions by prohibiting headers in games and practices for younger players will nonetheless never solve the problem that the players must still be trained to do headers safely and properly. So, when at an older age they are allowed access to headers, the players have often gained fear of concussions before gaining the necessary skills, meaning an increased concussion rate may actually end up being the unintended consequence of an attempted safety reform.

Another bane for the year-round-pay-to-play system would be the institution of appropriate rest periods, which would allow teen athletes to participate in multiple high-school sports for invaluable cross training and socialization. Fewer games, less practice time, shorter seasons, fewer tournaments, but also less revenue for the pay-to-play industry underwritten by its punishing schedules. This is why the push for change will almost surely have to come from the outside.

There are ongoing attempts at the NCAA and national SafeSport organizational level to research and intervene to also protect the mental health of athletes. But the reach of these efforts is still limited. Unfortunately, our mental-health system, much like the rest of our nation's healthcare system, is most easily accessed by the wealthier members of society.

The pay-to-play sports families are the families who are most likely to be able to afford mental-health care for their children, so let's start at this access point and expand beyond it. What if there were training and resources available to licensed mental-health professionals as well as coaches to detect easily and readily in their youth-athlete patients signs of competition distress, burnout, and overinvolvement from parents? What if club coaches, directors, or mental-game coaches had to admit that competition stress and parental overinvolvement was doing harm to a child? Would they be in a position to suggest that perhaps the paying customer should no longer be playing? The answer is likely no.

So, neutral mental-health professionals should be the only ones allowed to provide direct mental-health guidance to youth athletes and their parents. These professionals would not be employed by the clubs, the sports-governing bodies, or any of the various Youth Sports Industry–affiliated businesses. Let's say parents of a youth athlete ask a neutral mental-health professional to work on their child's sports-related confidence. The first goal upon which an agreement would need to be reached between parents, the child, and the clinician before work could proceed would be if, in fact, that athlete should continue to play the game and under what conditions? Even if the confidence level improved, should the athlete be allowed to exit the game? Neutral mental-health professionals could play a critical role in assessing the adherence to mental-health-promotion practices such as the Children's Bill of Rights in Sports when national sports-governing bodies and their affiliates are going through proposed accreditation processes. An independent mental-health professional's perspective on the social-emotional risks associated with youth sports would allow for the inclusion of developmentally healthy, whole person–centered mission statements and practices in national, state, and local youth-sports organizations.

But, what highly trained, hardworking, overburdened, and often modestly paid mental-health professional might not be tempted to get in on the gravy train by joining in the Youth Sports Industry goals of win now, more is better, and keep the families believing and traveling, no matter the cost? After all, who could argue with the laudable goals of increasing motivation, building confidence, and managing stress to improve performance? A layperson might easily imagine what the profit-driven guidelines are from the insurance companies who employ licensed mental-health professionals to "evaluate" whether a higher level of care for a patient in crisis is needed. The unspoken rule: Aggressively dissuade the more expensive, longer-term care and engage a Dr. No.

In the Youth Sports Industry, the strategy would likely be hire a Dr. Yes. Vulnerable individuals and parents will pay enormous amounts of money if they believe Dr. Yes when Dr. Yes hints at offering a mental-game product guaranteed to improve their child's sports performance and life. Youth athletes' lives have often become desperate when the dream of fame and prestige does not appear to be coming true, especially when mental health has been ignored or discarded along the way by those employed by the industry which loves to rationalize behind closed doors that "it is just a business." The ends of the Youth Sports Industry's bottom line are more often than not used to justify the means in the actions and minds of those who are in it to make money or win only without considering the ethics and impact of their practices upon these athletes. Enforced mandates with the consequences of income loss, certification loss, banning from the sport, and potentially prison if the mandates are not followed are the only things that hold out any hope of stopping the dangerous practices, but the greed and hubris involved on the part of many in the industry are formidable foes.

Major reforms have occurred in sports in the United States, as, for example, in the changing age and body type to an older and more muscular build prescribed to elite female gymnasts. This was a change from prior efforts to severely restrict weight gain and delay puberty to allow very young, pixie-like female athletes to compete at Olympic levels. Nonetheless, coaching practices that facilitate eating disorders in athletes run rampant. To be applauded is a recent change in the nationally renowned University of Oregon track program, which makes DEXA body-fat scanning an optional-only practice for the runners, and the reporting of the individual test results to the coaches will no longer be permitted. The potentially helpful aspects for the athlete of these optional medical-scan findings can only be reported to the medical professional and dietician who helps interpret them to the athlete. Restricting access to the test information is a more appropriate division of roles between coaches, athletes, and medical professionals and helps to avoid dual-role conflicts. The new rule can hopefully provide a protective boundary between how the athlete views and acts upon these voluntary test results and how the coach might have misused the results as a training tool in the past.[39]

Clearly the need for overuse-injury prevention has arrived for a broad swath of youth-sports participants who are not training at the college or Olympic level but whose injury rate and age of injury is nothing less than astonishing. The need for reform could not be clearer to those families who have stayed in the Youth Sports Industry for long enough and with multiple children to see the rapidly accelerating injury trends of the type that keep an athlete on the sidelines for years or for good. It is the responsibility of professionals to be critical of such preventable injury trends and to demand change. Many parents will join this movement, but professional intervention is required precisely because there remains a subset of parents who are pushing the more-is-better model.

Insurance Companies

The Youth Sports Industry will change if failing to do so threatens its profits, and one scenario could work. If health-insurance companies eventually grow weary of the astronomical cost of stitching back together young athletes and start to change the rules of what is covered—and if they can show that the injury resulted from overuse—clubs might be viewed as complicit and thus liable. Some would argue that the overuse epidemic is a public-health emergency considering how many resources are devoted to fixing injuries that could have been prevented.

Many health-insurance providers go to extraordinary lengths to nickel and dime mental-health care providers for services desperately needed by their policyholders. So it is surprising that health-insurance companies have not turned their attention to the issue of overuse injuries in young athletes. Surely they have internal data showing that they are spending much more today than they were ten, twenty, and especially thirty years ago to repair devastating sports injuries to youth. The basic business model of most health-insurance companies rests on the premiums from the many healthy individuals, especially youth, covering those in need of expensive healthcare costs. But the cost of repairing an anterior cruciate ligament (ACL) tear in a youth athlete is hardly insignificant; it ranges between $20,000 and $50,000. So why do health-insurance companies continue to shoulder such costs?

For those families without insurance or even without Cadillac-level insurance, a major injury such as an ACL tear could devastate the family's finances to the point that they should think twice about having their child conform to the rigorous, year-round practice schedule dictated by most pay-to-play clubs. For families with Cadillac-level health insurance, the out-of-pocket expense tends to be minor, but what about the trauma experienced by the young athlete who not only faces surgery but somewhere in the range of a year of rehabilitation.

If the health-insurance providers were to make it clear that their policies would not pay for overuse injuries in youth athletes, this could provide such a shock to the Youth Sports Industry that it could lead to fundamental reform, at least in the area of practice and game schedules. Clubs not being able require as many practices and games also cannot charge as much so they will resist such reforms.

There is always some ambiguity when it comes to diagnosing an overuse injury. But a 2019 report in *Science Daily*[40] states that the "first evidence of ACL injuries is in repetitive knee stress and failure to accommodate sufficient rest between periods of strenuous exercise, which may be key factors behind the rapid rise in anterior cruciate ligament [ACL] injuries in world sport."[41] Dalton's 1992 study on overuse injuries in adolescent athletes suggested that up to 50 percent of youth-sports injuries were potentially related to overuse.[42] If health-insurance companies subpoenaed the practice, game, and tournament schedule of a club for which a young athlete played, they could, with backing from physicians, make a strong case that the injury resulted from overuse and be justified in denying coverage to repair it. Additionally, surgeons can often tell when an injury results from overuse, which would also be a basis for denying coverage.

Health-insurance companies could deal a powerful blow to the overuse-injury epidemic by making clear that their coverage will not extend to young athletes playing for clubs that are not certified as following reasonable schedules. The trickiest part is that many youth athletes participate in activities in the same sport sponsored by multiple organizations in addition to their pay-to-play club team. Still, where there is a will, there is a way. Guidelines could be set for all organizations and clubs that if not followed would result in health-insurance companies not paying to repair overuse injuries.

The upper 1 percent of families with children in pay-to-play sports might shrug at the fact that health-insurance companies would no longer pay the costs of repairing overuse injuries. They might view the $20,000 to $50,000 in costs for surgery to repair ACL tears, even in the instance of multiple tears and repairs, to be simply one of the costs necessary to earn preferential admission to college. But for the other 99 percent of families, this would likely be such a shock that parents would have to think through the wisdom, and the financial risk, of more and more and more practices and games.

Additionally, clubs might well find themselves the subject of lawsuits, which could help put an end to their longstanding practice of externalizing the costs of the overuse injuries for which they are substantially responsible. Nonprofits do not enjoy immunity from lawsuits. Health-insurance companies could also draw more attention to the epidemic of overuse injuries by publicizing the data they have and highlighting the increasing collateral damage that the professionalization of youth sports is causing that might serve as a wakeup call for change.

In the meantime, however, insurance companies are developing a different niche that speaks to how downright bizarre elements of the Youth Sports Industry have become. Annual player fees for pay-to-play clubs, which tend to be several thousand dollars, are almost never refundable. If, for example, a player joins a club in May, the parents must sign a contract to pay one year's worth of fees. And the family is obligated to pay these fees even if at the very first team practice in

May the player suffers a devastating injury that will keep him or her off the field for the remaining twelve months of the year. Numerous insurance companies now offer policies that, should the player sustain an injury, pay out claims to cover the player fees on a prorated basis.

Professional Athletes

The influence that famous professional athletes have is immense, though they do not always set the best example. Followers of the United States Men's National Soccer Team were exposed to an unseemly spectacle in the aftermath of the 2022 World Cup. In revenge for publicly leaked critical remarks made by national team coach Gregg Berhalter about Gio Reyna, the Reyna parents asked the United States Soccer Federation to look into a decades old incident between Berhalter and his then-girlfriend, now wife, alleging that abuse had taken place which should disqualify Berhalter as the U.S. head coach. It was interesting what came out next. Fans learned that Gio's father, Claudio Reyna, a United States Men's Soccer Team legend with easy access to coaches, had long been pressuring junior national team and national team coaches alike to give Gio more playing time. It turned out that the absurd dynamic that takes place daily across the country of overinvolved parents pressuring coaches was taking place at the highest levels of United States soccer.

Nonetheless, professional athletes could play a critical role in reforming what ails youth sports today. Their public influence could be used to promote a dramtic change in bringing youth sports to all. What if, instead of building and paying for youth recreational centers in one neighborhood and placing their names on it, they could form a powerful pro-athlete lobby to pass federal laws to require states to fund youth recreation facilities in every community across socio-economic levels? Many have begun to endorse strategic national athlete empowerment movements, such as Project Play's Child Athlete's Bill of Rights.

More and more Olympic and professional athletes such as Michael Phelps and Simone Biles are speaking out about the dire need for training at the elite level to prioritize the athlete's physical and mental health given the extreme performance demands, pressure, and identity-development challenges that athletes face. Famous athletes such as Crystal Dunn, a current member of the United States Women's National Team, are telling all who will listen about how limiting, in terms of who can afford to play, the current American youth-soccer system is, and this is true for many other sports.

Some Cy Young award-winning pitchers refuse to do any pitching training for youth baseball players, who should be resting their arms in the off-season. It is heartening to see the emergence of the Bridge City Soccer Academy for girls in Portland, Oregon, spearheaded by former United States Women's National Team and Olympian Shannon Boxx, who hopes to bring the fun back into sports. Imagine if there were mandates that required all youth-sports clubs to follow best prescribed practices.

Taylor Twellman, a national team–level soccer player whose career was ended prematurely by concussions, has become arguably the best American announcer of professional soccer matches, including MLS games. He is also a keen commentator on the state of soccer overall in the United States. In a January 2022 tweet, Twellman had this to say about an Instagram post, which he included in his tweet, by a parent proudly detailing the insane schedule of a U-12 girls team that included 14 games in 17 days, as well as trips to Chicago, San Diego, Dallas, Boston, and Richmond: "You read this and tell me if youth soccer is 'healthy' in this country."

What if these pro athletes' examples were publicized to the highest degree and their endorsements of clubs that are affordable and allow for protecting the health of the players were placed front and center on club websites? What if famous basketball players like LeBron James endorsed local, one-season-per-year of play only for the broad-based development of up-and-coming basketball players? What if young, world-class, American professional soccer players like Christain Pulisic endorsed new training technology that could detect when a youth's ligaments and body mechanics were in need of a more specialized training regime to prevent injury in all levels of developing youth-soccer players? One could imagine many players and parents getting on board the pro athlete train's demands for healthy sport developmental trends.

Epilogue

The Youth Sports Industry marches on. But lately there have been developments that have resulted in more and more people asking questions about the legitimacy of the single most important driver of the Youth Sports Industry, namely preferential admission to college.

Whatever one thinks of the July 2023 Supreme Court decision curtailing affirmative action in college admissions, it is leading to an examination of numerous other factors beyond academic merit that feature in college admissions, including the preferential treatment of athletes. Why should athletics have anything to do with college admissions? In most of the rest of the world, where admission to higher education is often decided by examinations, it does not play any role.

In the United States, however, athletics is often the deciding factor in determining whether or not someone is admitted to an elite college. Furthermore, it is often the case that athletes applying to elite colleges also fall into the category of legacy, in other words having had a relative who attended the college. If the societal conversation about the appropriateness of athletes and legacies enjoying preferential admission to colleges shifts in a critical direction, then change will likely result. Maybe without the pressure of performing so as to win admission to the "right" college, kids could return to playing sports mainly for fun.

Endnotes

Chapter 1

1. O'Sullivan, John. *Changing the Game*, New York, NY: Morgan James Publishing, 2014.

2. Gleason, Scott. Hope Solo says Youth Soccer in the U.S. has become a "rich, white-kid sport." *USA Today*, June 28, 2018.

3. Center for Disease Control and Prevention, Childhood Obesity Facts, Prevalence of Obesity in the United States, 2019, *cdc.gov*

4. Mulcahy, Glen. 2019. Why do kids play video games? Paradigmsports.ca (March21): https://www.paradigmsports.ca/why-do-kids-play-video-games/. Accessed October 5, 2021.

5. Brenner, J.S., American Academy of Pediatrics Council on Sports Medicine and Fitness. Overuse injuries, overtraining, and burnout in child and adolescent athletes. *Pediatrics*, 200, 119(6): 1242–1245, June 2007. Reaffirmed 2014.

6. Smith, N.A.; Thiphalak, C.; Hulyun, X. Soccer-Related Injuries Treated in Emergency Departments: 1990–2014. *Pediatrics*, 138, //doi.org/10.1542/peds2016 -0346

7. Twenge J.M.; Cooper, A.B.; Joiner, T.E.; Duffy, M.E.; Binau, S.G. (2019). Age, period, and cohort trends in mood-disorder indicators and suicide-related outcomes in a nationally representative data set, 2005–2017, *Journal of Abnormal Psychology*, 128(3), 185–199.

8. Jeff Passan. *The Arm: Inside the Billion-Dollar Mystery of the Most Valuable Commodity in Sports*, Harper-Collins, 2016.

9. Joan Ryan, *Little Girls in Pretty Boxes: The Making and Breaking of Elite Gymnasts and Figure Skaters*, Grand Central Publishing, 1996.

10. Gregory, Sean., KID Sports INC. "How your child's rec league turned into a $15 billion industry," *Time* magazine, September 4, 2017.

11. Gray, Peter. *Free to Learn Why Unleashing the Instinct to Play Will Make Our Children Happier, More Self-Reliant, and Better Students for Life*, New York: Basic Books, 2013.

12. NCAA Student Athlete Well Being Study, May 2020, https://www.ncaa.org/news/2020/5/22/survey-shows-student-athletes-grappling-with-mental-health-issues.aspx

13. Barrett, Ruth. "The Mad, Mad World of Niche Sports in Ivy League–Obsessed Parents," *The Atlantic*, 74–85, November 2020.

14. Project Play. State of play 2018: Trends and development. The Aspen Institute, November 7, 2018, https://www.aspeninstitute.org/wp-content/uploads/2018/10/StateofPlay2018_v4WEB_2-FINAL.pdf

15. Notte, Jason. "Here are the best sports for a college scholarship," MarketWatch. https://www.marketwatch.com/story/these-are-the-sports-your-child-should-play-to-get-a-college-scholarship-2017-05-08.

16. NCAA estimated probability of competing in college athletics, 2020. https://www.ncaa.org/about/resources/research/estimated-probability-competing-college-athletics

Chapter 2

17. https://cdn1.sportngin.com/attachments/document/2cf1-2160365/2019-2020_ECNL_Member_Club_Handbook.pdf. Accessed April 22, 2020.

18. https://docs.google.com/document/d/1RHzxlD22CcWACfq4pywx65SBT19sP_Ks4hW4KVua7_Q/edit/ Accessed April 22, 2020.

Chapter 3

19. http://www.usyouthsoccer.org/assets/1/36/playerdevelopmentmodel_smith_(1).pdf?595. Accessed 20 April, 2021.

20. Farrey, Tom. *Game On: The All-American Race to Make Champions of Our Children*, New York, NY: ESPN Books, 2008.

Chapter 4

21. Project Play, 2015. *Sports for all. Play for life. A playbook to get every kid in the game.* https://www.aspeninstitute.org/wp-content/uploads/2015/01/Aspen -Institute-Project-Play-Report.pdf.

22. Online Etymology Dictionary. https://etymonline.com.

23. NCAA Research, 2020. https://ncaaorg.s3.amazonaws.com/research/pro _beyond/2020RES_ProbabilityBeyondHSFiguresMethod.pdf

24. Coakley, J. "Organized Youth Sports: Whose Interests Do They Serve?" *Sports in Society Issues and Controversies*, 13th ed., 82–119), McGraw Hill, 2021.

25. "Cost of Youth Sports Delaying Retirement for Parents," Businesswire, 2019. https://www.businesswire.com/news/home/20190515005052/en/Cost-of -Youth-Sports-Delaying-Retirement-for-Parents

26. USA Hockey. "10 years ago today: USA Hockey approves American Development Model, January 18, 2019. https://www.usahockey.com/news_article /show/986127

27. Dunn, R., Dorsch, T.E., King, M.Q. & Rothlisberger, K.J. (2016). The Impact of Family Financial Investment on Perceived Parent Pressure and Child Enjoyment and Commitment in Organized Youth Sport. *Family Relations: An Interdisciplinary Journal of Applied Family Studies*, 65(2), 287–299. https://doi.org/10.1111 /fare.12193

Chapter 5

28. Farrey, T. *Game On*, New York, NY: ESPN Books, 2008, pp. 81–82.

29. https://www.aspenprojectplay.org/childrens-rights-and-sports

30. Eckstein, R. *How College Athletics Are Hurting Girls' Sports: The Pay-to-Play Pipleline*, Rowman & Littlefield, 2017.

31. Farrey, T. *Game On*, p. 145.

32. Eckstein, R. *How College Athletics Are Hurting Girls' Sports: The Pay-to-Play Pipeline*, p. 74.

33. Shulman, J.L.; Brown, W.G. *The Game of Life: College Sports and Educational Values*, Princeton University Press, 2001.

34. Anderson, N., and Svrluga., B. "Varsity Athletes, Admissions, and Enrollment at Top Colleges," *The Washington Post*, June 12, 2019. https://www.washingtonpost .com education/2019/06/12/varsity-athletes-admissions-enrollment-top-colleges/

35. https://uscenterforsafesport.org/

36. Brenner, J.S. "Overuse Injuries, Overtraining, and Burnout in Child and Adolescent Athletes, *Pediatrics,* 2007, 119:1242–1245.

37. Brenner, 2007, p. 1245.

38. https://www.stopsportsinjuries.org/STOP/About/STOP/About/STOP_Sports_Injuries.aspx?hkey=7404718a-bf38-4936-acb8-a2a146f5045a

39. Goe, K. "University of Oregon Athletic Programs Cannot Monitor Athletes' Weight, Body Fat," *The Oregonian*, December 3, 2021, B3.

40. Chen, J., Kim, J., Shao, W., Schlecht, S.H., Baek, S.Y., Jones, A.K., Ahn, T., Ashton-Miller, J., Holl, M.M.B., Wojtys, E.M. "An Anterior Cruciate Ligament Failure Mechanism," *The American Journal of Sports Medicine,* 2019, 47 (9): 2067 DOI: 10.1177/0363546519854450.

41. Monash University. "Kneeding a Break: First Evidence ACL Injuries an Overuse Failure," *ScienceDaily*, July 23, 2019. www.sciencedaily.com/releases/2019/07/190723110518.htm

42. Dalton, S.E. "Overuse Injuries in Adolescent Athletes," *Sports Medicine,* 1992, 13:58–70.

About the Authors

Jean Linscott, Ph.D., is a clinical child psychologist. She has been working professionally with children and families for over thirty years in hospital-based, clinic, and private-practice settings. She and Kenneth Ruoff are the parents of three athletes who are veterans of the Youth Sports Industry.

Kenneth Ruoff, Ph.D., is a professor of history at Portland State University and the author of numerous award-winning books. From the perspective of a historian, he is astonished, in comparison to what he experienced as a kid, at how drastically different a youth-sports environment his family has faced these past two decades.

www.ingramcontent.com/pod-product-compliance
Lightning Source LLC
Chambersburg PA
CBHW020238130626
46549CB00005B/1957